River of Memory:
Dharma Chronicles

Series Ganesha Press

ABOUT GANESHA PRESS
Ganesha Press is the publishing house of Dechen, an international association of Sakya and Kagyu Buddhist centres and groups founded by Lama Jampa Thaye under the authority of Karma Thinley Rinpoche.

Other books by Lama Jampa Thaye

A Garland of Gold
Diamond Sky
Way of Tibetan Buddhism
Wisdom in Exile
Rain of Clarity

River of Memory:

Dharma Chronicles

2nd Edition

Lama Jampa Thaye

RABSEL
PUBLICATIONS

RABSEL PUBLICATIONS
16, rue de Babylone
76430 La Remuée, France
www.rabsel.com
contact@rabsel.com

© Rabsel Publications, La Remuée, France, 2021
ISBN 978-2-36017-043-2

Dedicated to my masters

Contents

Preface by
Karma Thinley Rinpoche

ༀ། འཕེན་ཟམཝ་ལས་ནཟར་ནཉིས་འཛོམས་མཁས་རབ་ཀྱི། ཕུང་ལོ་ཉི་ཤུ་ར་འདག་གིས་སྐུ་བན་སྐྱབས་སོ་ཁག ངར་འཕྱུར་འཛ
ཟསྦུ་ན་རཝེ་ལེགས་ཆོག་ལ་འརྒྱེ། སྐུ་ མ་ཚུམ་ས་ མ་མཁར་ཡར་མཆོན་སྩུན་སྐྱོགས། གཝར་ཟཝ་ངཝ་ར་ད་མ་ཛེ་མད་ད་ནཟར་ས
ངར་ཤྱར་ཤྱར་ཟཝེ་རེ་ཕོ་ལོས་ཕེ་ངལ་བསྲུ། དུ་ཛྱེ་ཕོ་གས་ཕུལ་གཏ་ནུ་ངུ་ར་ཀྲ་ཆོམ་ཆེ་ར་ནཝོ། ཕྱོག་ད་ཕེ་སྐྱ་ནཁོ་
ཀྱུ་ཀྱེ་པ་དོར་ཀྲོག་ལ་ནུ། ཆེ་ལ་ཕར། ཀྲུལ་རངར་ ནཟུ་སྒུག་ ཀལ་ལུ་ ནཟ་ཀ་ཆ་ སྤོ་ སཝ་ནཝེ་པ་ནཝར། ཟཝ་སྐུག་ སྐྱ་རལ་ ས
རཝ་སྤུལ་ སྐྱུ་ རྟེ་ ནཟ་ནཝ་ཝ་ དརར་ཤྱར་ ནཟོ་ནཝེ་ སྨེ་ པོ་ ནཟར་ནཝར་ཛ་ མ་ ཟཝ་ནྒུ་ པ་ཟ། ༢༠༢༠ ཆོ་ ད་ར་པ་རར་ ཟོ་ དུ་ཕ་ ཆོ་ མ་ དཀ

The master scholar, rich in merit and good deeds,
Who, at the age of twenty, received from me the vows of
  refuge etc,
And who has well benefited the teachings by giving many
  initiations and transmissions,
Is the renowned Lama Jampa Thaye.

Furthermore, having excellently met with many holy teachers,
And having fastened the thread on the jewel rosary of the
  initiation and transmission lineage,
He rained down the dharma on trainees across England and
  other lands.
Thus it is my wish that all should study his newly written book.

*Having received the title '4ᵗʰ Karma Thinley' from the mouth of the
16ᵗʰ Gyalwang Lord [Karmapa, 1924–1981], and recognized as a tulku
in the presence of Dakshul Thinley [40ᵗʰ Sakya Trichen, 1871–1935]
with the name 'Wangdu Norbu Nyingpo', I wrote this on the auspicious day of my ninetieth year, the year 2020. May it be virtuous.*

Introduction

The story of Buddhism goes back two-and-a-half millennia, but the story of Buddhism in the West is more recent. As the dharma unfolded in Asia, the genius of Buddha manifested in various lines of transmission. Now, this teaching and these traditions, including the four Vajrayana schools of Tibet – Sakya, Kagyu, Geluk and Nyingma – have come to the West.

At the heart of each of these traditions is simply the direct transmission of dharma from one person to another. The traditions – with their monastic institutions, colleges and retreat centres – are merely the structure built around this process. Consequently, it has been customary for practitioners to preserve detailed records of the initiations, reading-transmissions and instructions that they have received from their teachers. If, in due course, they themselves are given teaching responsibilities, such accounts assure the integrity of the process of transmission, an integrity that is crucial if the dharma is to retain its transformative force.

In a sense, *River of Memory* is a modern version of this type of work, describing how I was educated in dharma by my two principal masters, H.H. Sakya Gongma Trichen and Karma Thinley Rinpoche, as well as a number of others, most importantly H.H. Karmapa. Since I remained a lay-man, this education was not as highly structured as one received within the monastic system. Nevertheless, it possessed four major elements of such a training: receiving and maintaining vows, receiving textual teachings, obtaining Vajrayana initiations and practising meditation.

Consequently, these four elements are the principal focus of this present history. Yet it also chronicles something of the wider context in which my education took place, since the dharma, though its essence is timeless, is always received and transmitted by people who are themselves embedded in a particular culture and a certain historical period. So it is a kind of series of snapshots of Buddhism in the West, taken from a particular angle. However, it should be admitted that although the teachers and teachings described here were truly profound, the student who has chronicled them was merely someone who was drifting from scene to scene.

I have been asked a number of times to write such an account, and in fact an earlier version of this work appeared in 2005. Now, however, this updated and more extensive edition has been prepared for publication, with the assistance of my wife, Albena, and my editor, Benjamin Lister. Thanks also to Adrian O'Sullivan, Jetsunma Rigzin Khandro, Kunga Gyaltsen, David Armstrong, Gill Bennett and Hannah Lister.

Lama Jampa Thaye
London, 2020

Chapter One
Beginning Again

Sometimes it can seem that our lifetimes are as brief as dew drops in the morning sun. They have hardly started when they come to an end. Yet each life is merely one in a beginningless series, where we are propelled forwards by our deeds. Maybe this explains why I met the dharma in this life.

I was born near Manchester in 1952 to Catholic parents; my brother was born four years later. Our ancestry was mostly Irish, though our family name is an old Northern English one. My father's parents were mill workers from East Manchester, both of whom died before my birth. During the war, my father, a quiet and gentle man, had served in the ambulance corps, and so, when it was over, he took up nursing. It was during his training at Bolton Royal Infirmary that he met my mother, who came from a family living near Blackburn but which had more distant roots in southern Ireland via Liverpool.

After their marriage, my father was forced to become a factory-worker to support the family, while my mother gave up nursing to stay at home to raise us. It must have been tough for them; our first house lacked hot water, and national food rationing did not end until I was two years old. Britain was broke after the war and in debt to the U.S.A. The emperor had been reborn as a servant – a sharp lesson in the suffering of change.

In my early years, I was serious about the religious teachings that I heard at church and school. However, there was another element present in my life, which would eventually dissolve my adherence to Catholicism. From about the age of seven onwards, I experienced flashes of the dream-like and illusory nature of things. They convinced me that there was another reality, beyond this shadowy world. It couldn't be captured in concept or language, and yet I felt that it had been our true nature from time without beginning. Often I would feel intimations of its presence – sometimes blissful, at other times overwhelming – when roaming in the open fields beyond our terrace housing and the iron-foundry, cotton mill and paint factory that surrounded us.

My first school, St Charles R.C. Primary School, was followed by De La Salle College, a Direct Grant Grammar school in Salford – the kind of place that was a route out and upwards for working-class boys who could pass exams. It was an institution that was uncompromising in its intellectual toughness and did not sell us short. I haunted the school library, reading everything I could get my hands on. It is only now that I understand what we have lost with the disappearance of such institutions.

I had heard of Buddhism here and there, but it took me a little while to make the connection between its teaching and my own glimpses of that other reality. My admiration for the songs of Bob Dylan had led me to his immediate literary predecessors in the Beat Generation – writers such as Jack Kerouac and Allen Ginsberg – and their novels and poetry alerted me to the works of D.T. Suzuki and other Buddhist authors. There I found, in the explanations of emptiness, something that was so familiar from my experiences that it caused me to recognise the Buddha's teachings as my natural home. It was clear that I would never be able to return to Christianity: that had just been something I was passing through. Yet, at the same time, I understood that ideas and books about Buddhism were insufficient: one must actually live the Buddhist life, and so acquire the qualities of wisdom and compassion to which the teachings point. It would take me some years and a few bad turns to find that life.

In 1968, filled with impatience and in a hurry to find the world of Kerouac's *Dharma Bums,* I left home and education to spend the next four years moving around between Manchester and London. I must have lived in about fifteen places during that time, often sleeping on people's floors or couches. At least there was usually a guitar, even if there wasn't much else. It was always a struggle, not least because I was four or five years younger than everybody around me.

Despite searching, I didn't discover much evidence of the spiritual life. Where I had thought it might be, I found just foolishness, including my own. Friends arrived, friends disappeared: some to politics, some to death and some leaving no forwarding address. Only one or two made it through later to serious dharma practice.

Although I visited the London Buddhist Society from time to time during those years, it was some time before I grasped that there could be no neutral ground between Buddhism and Bohemia. Finally, however, I came to understand that either I could embrace the dharma, or I could sink down to the bottom of a world full of lies. I had no other choice but to start again at the beginning with the dharma – but properly, this time.

When I think about it now, I can see that it was the experiences in my childhood that had really impelled me to dharma. It was not all that much to do with the atmosphere of the times: that was just the background, some seemingly supportive scenery but nothing more. However, I can also see that the dharma had at least landed in the West for me to discover. At another time and in another place, that might not have been the case. So one might say that the inner and outer conditions were aligned.

In December 1972, I joined The Manchester University Buddhist Society, and also began to attend the meditation classes of the Theravada teacher Russell Williams, who had been there from the beginning of the society in 1952. From then on, I never looked back at the scene I had left, but, thanks to Russell's clear and kind guidance, I immediately established a daily routine of practice and study. In the same month, I gained a provisional place to read Religious Studies at the University, with the vague aim of becoming a school-teacher. I felt that such a career might give me a suitable worldly basis for a life focussed on the dharma.

I was one of the six percent of my generation who would be awarded a University place that year. The course would begin the following autumn and admission was contingent upon completing my previously abandoned A-level studies – something that I hoped would please my long-suffering parents. It was the least I could do for them.

I was certainly fortunate that it was a world in which I could pick up my studies again. It was a world that had been built, over the generations, both by the famous heroes and leaders and by countless unsung men and women – the factory-worker, the small businessman, the conserver, the reformer, the farmer and the teacher, the policeman and the priest – all the people we had despised in our 'alternative society'. Now was the time for respect and gratitude for their labours.

Within six months, the direction of my newly-established dharma-practice shifted towards the Mahayana ('Great Vehicle'), after I heard about a Tibetan scholar called Geshe Tsultrim Gyaltsen. He was one of the handful of Tibetan lamas resident in Britain, and was giving classes at his home in London. Intrigued, I decided to attend, taking an old friend with me. It was my first encounter, outside of books, with Tibetan Buddhism. Geshe Tsultrim, who lived with his English wife in an apartment in Muswell Hill, was particularly learned in the Gelug tradition, and, although his English was far from perfect, his teaching on the compassion and wisdom of the bodhisattva path drew me towards the Mahayana.

As the fourteenth-century master, Tokme Zangpo, says:

Now you have gained this boat of freedom and
    endowment,
You should study, reflect and meditate
To row yourself and all beings across the ocean of
    samsara.
Such is the practice of a bodhisattva.

Yet, as I did not live in London, studying Mahayana seriously with Geshe Tsultrim did not appear feasible. However, there were two recently established Tibetan meditation centres where it was possible to stay for extended periods of time: Kham House in Essex and Kagyu Samye Ling in the Scottish Borders. So, thinking that these offered possibilities for the kind of studies for which I was searching, I decided to visit both, going first to Kham House in early July. There, the disarming friendliness of the resident lama, Radha Chime Rinpoche, drew me to his Karma-Kagyu tradition.

Three weeks later, I travelled to Samye Ling. This centre, named after the first monastery established in Tibet, had been founded in 1967 by Trungpa Rinpoche and Akong Rinpoche. It had, however, been through a number of difficulties, culminating in a rift between its two founders. Eventually, Trungpa Rinpoche had departed for North America, leaving Akong Tulku in sole charge.

In the summer of 1973, Samye Ling consisted of a large country house with various adjacent buildings, set in the damp Dumfriesshire countryside. The turbulence of its first few years had given way to a more serious atmosphere. Consequently, it appeared to be a place where one could receive some instruction. Akong Tulku was in residence, together with an old friend of his, Karma Thinley Rinpoche, who was staying in the centre for a few weeks after fulfilling an engagement at Edinburgh University.

It was a couple of the centre's students who told me something of this second lama's background. Born in Eastern Tibet in 1931, he had been recognised as the rebirth of Biru Kunrik, an important lama of the Sakya school, one of the four major Tibetan Buddhist traditions; two decades later, H.H. the 16th Gyalwa Karmapa, head of the Karma-Kagyu school, would name him fourth in line of the fifteenth-century scholar, Karma Thinleypa. Rinpoche was trained by a number of eminent masters such as Khangsar Khenpo, Ngawang Yonten Gyamtso, a rather unconventional lama from the Sakya tradition. In 1959, after some time at the monastery of Tsurphu in central Tibet, where he received full monastic ordination, Rinpoche left for India in the party of refugees led by H.H. Karmapa, fleeing from Chinese Communist oppression.

In India, Rinpoche had served as a tutor at The Young

Lamas' Home School, established in Delhi by Freda Bedi, the Oxford graduate turned Indian freedom-fighter also known as Sister Palmo. Subsequently, he accepted the post of abbot at the Kagyu nunnery near Dharamsala, which had also been set up by the remarkable Mrs Bedi. During these years, Rinpoche managed to continue with his own education, receiving the noted Sakya teaching known as *The Path and its Fruit* from H.H. Sakya Trizin, the head of that school. He also received, during that period, *The Treasury of Spiritual Instructions* from the meditation-master Kalu Rinpoche. Finally, in 1971, at the suggestion of his own teachers, Rinpoche had emigrated to Toronto, in order to act as spiritual guide for some of the Tibetans who had recently been granted admission as refugees by the Canadian government.

Rinpoche was not particularly busy during his time at Samye Ling that summer. He was, however, giving some classes, which I decided to attend. As I listened to Rinpoche teach in his heavily-accented English, it was obvious both that he was very learned and that he had no intention of selling out to the modern world. He looked like the kind of teacher that I needed.

Within a week of meeting Rinpoche, I requested him to give me Refuge, the formal admission to the Buddhist path, in which one goes for 'refuge' to the Three Jewels of the Buddha, the Dharma and the Sangha, taking them as one's teacher, one's path and one's companions on the path, respectively. The very next day, he performed this ceremony, giving me the name Karma Jampa Thaye.

After this ceremony, Rinpoche gave me the reading-transmission for the *Chariot that Draws us along the Noble Way*, composed in the sixteenth century by the 9th Karmapa, Wangchuk Dorje. Such a reading-transmission (in Tibetan *lung*) conveys the power that has been present in the teaching from the time of its original formulation, and, by receiving it, one is able to practise the instructions contained in the text as part of one's spiritual path. In this case, this particular liturgical text contained the preliminary set of meditations for the *Mahamudra* ('The Great Seal') precepts of the Kagyu tradition.

As elaborated by mediaeval Indian tantric masters, such as Saraha and Tilopa, this contemplative system teaches both that all appearances of the phenomenal world are simply aspects of mental experience and that mind itself also lacks any intrinsic nature, being empty like space. Hence, all phenomena, outer and inner, are, in actuality, 'sealed' by emptiness, in that emptiness of intrinsic nature is their ultimate reality. Through meditating on this view, to which he is introduced by his master, the *Mahamudra* yogin is liberated from the mistaken perception that assigns a fictitious substantiality to the duality of a solid, independent subjective self and an equally solid world of objects. It is this misperception that is the underlying cause of the selfish emotions that perpetuate the sufferings of samsara, since it forces us to read the world through the prism of self against other, rather than, as it actually is, a fluidity in which self and other, subject and object, are mutually interdependent. With the ending of our entrapment in this cycle of misperception, the state of Buddhahood, characterised by unrestricted wisdom and compassion, is attained.

To approach the heart of this practice, one needs to prepare oneself experientially by completing the series of outer and inner preliminaries, as detailed in the 9th Karmapa's text. Therefore, following Rinpoche's departure from Britain, at the beginning of September, I would start on the first major section, comprising one hundred thousand refuge prayers and physical prostrations, to-

CHAPTER ONE - BEGINNING AGAIN

gether with the verses for generating bodhichitta, the altruistic resolve to achieve Buddhahood for the benefit of all. In the first year, I managed to complete this initial section and the subsequent practice of meditation on Vajrasattva. Since this deity embodies the primordial purity of mind, this second stage dissolves obstructions to spiritual progress caused by the prior breakage of vows and the commission of non-virtuous actions.

Meanwhile, Rinpoche himself would be unable to return to Britain for almost four years, due to his need to establish residency in Canada and so acquire citizenship there. A lot would happen in that time. My University studies began, and, while my fellow Theology students were friendly, they were very different from the bohemians I had been around in the previous five years. Most of the professors and lecturers, for their part, looked like they would rather be in Oxford or Cambridge. Yet, despite my 'culture shock', I was content to settle down to do my time at University; I had no big plans or expectations.

As an auspicious sign, shortly after my University life started, I received the Individual Liberation Vow for lay-practitioners and the Bodhisattva Vow from Chime Rinpoche, both vows embodying major aspects of the moral training that underpins the meditative path and renders it genuinely altruistic. Specifically, the first Vow embodies a commitment to conduct that eschews any harm to others. The second Vow builds upon this with the commitment to strive for Buddhahood, the state possessing the supreme qualities of wisdom and compassion through which one can work to liberate all beings from sufferings. One can therefore see these two vows as the core of the Shravakayana and Mahayana respectively. It was good to have these foundations for my new life.

In June 1974, I met H.H. Sakya Trizin for the first time. His Holiness was the head of the Sakya tradition and the very same master from whom Rinpoche had received the transmission of the *Path and its Fruit*. He had been born into the Dolma Phodrang branch of the ruling Khon dynasty of Sakya in 1945, and had been trained, since early childhood, by some of the greatest contemporary masters of his school, including Dampa Rinpoche from Ngor monastery and Khenchen Jampal Zangpo. After going into exile in India at the age of thirteen, he had continued his education with the renowned scholar, Khenpo Appey. Now, he was staying in London for a few days, en route to America. The Buddhist Society, in concert with the Tibet Relief Fund, had arranged a reception in his honour at its headquarters in Eccleston Square. Luckily, I was able to attend this with Chime Rinpoche, who was related to His Holiness's wife, Dagmo Kushog-la. They both hailed from the province of Kham in East Tibet.

After a welcoming speech by the Society's president, Christmas Humphries, His Holiness gave a dharma talk in his clear English. I was very happy to be introduced to him over the tea and biscuits that followed. As I talked to His Holiness, I had the sense that he had all the time in the world; it was as if he came from a place that was simultaneously ancient and present, and I immediately felt a connection to him. Over time, His Holiness would become one of my two principal masters and his teachings would form the backbone of my spiritual practice. However, that would take a few years to become apparent.

His Holiness's brief stay in London was followed within two months by further induction into the Kagyu tradition, this time brought about by the visit of another of Karma Thinley Rinpoche's own lamas, Kalu Rinpoche,

Karma Rangjung Kunkhyap. This master, who had been trained in the 1920s and '30s at Palpung monastery in Eastern Tibet by great teachers such as Drubwang Norbu Dondrup and the 11th Situ Rinpoche, was making his second tour of the West. He was travelling with six young monks from the monastery that he had established in exile at Sonada, near Darjeeling in North-Eastern India.

After visiting Denmark and France, Kalu Rinpoche arrived at Kham House in early August with his monks and a melange of enthusiastic Western disciples, including his French interpreter, Denys Eysserie (later Lama Denys Dondrup), and Ole (later Lama Ole) and Hannah Nydahl. Somehow, Kalu Rinpoche, this small, almost bird-like ascetic figure, remained the still point around which this energy danced. It was clear to me that he was a major figure in the contemporary Kagyu world.

Once Kalu Rinpoche had settled into Kham House, he bestowed the initiation of the Buddha Amitabha from the Sky Dharma teachings of the seventeenth-century 'treasure revealer', Mingyur Dorje. Since the authority to meditate upon a particular deity, embodying enlightened qualities, is bestowed upon one by a master in such a ritual of initiation, it is indispensable for tantric practice. Thus it was my proper entry into Vajrayana, the 'uncommon' or 'extraordinary' Mahayana, and Kalu Rinpoche became my first 'vajra-master'.

A few days after this event, he was due to visit Samye Ling. The fact that his journey would take him quite close to Manchester provided me with a pretext to invite him to visit and give teachings. I explained to him that there were already a few people interested in Kagyu dharma in Manchester, since Chime Rinpoche had himself given a talk there and had supported the starting of a group, and, thus persuaded, Kalu Rinpoche agreed to my request.

A day later, therefore, we all travelled north. That evening, Kalu Rinpoche gave a teaching on the four thoughts that turn the mind to dharma: encouraging us to utilise our human life as a precious opportunity to practise dharma; to acknowledge the facts of impermanence and death in order to engage in the dharma without delay; to consider that, due to rebirth, our actions, virtuous or non-virtuous, will shape our future lives; and, finally, to contemplate the truth that, wherever one is born in the cycle of birth and death, there will be suffering, due to our habits of self-clinging and self-cherishing. As Kalu Rinpoche explained, these four reflections are the foundation of all progress on the spiritual path, since they generate in us a heart-felt wish for freedom, a freedom that can only come about through our turning to the dharma. In fact, I had already heard teachings on them from Karma Thinley Rinpoche the previous year, since the *four thoughts* actually constitute the 'outer' part of the *Mahamudra* preliminaries.

The venue that we had hired for the event was the Friends' Meeting House, located in the centre of Manchester, and a place where I had attended a meeting of the Theosophical Society several years before. Now, on this present occasion, one hundred people came to listen to Kalu Rinpoche's uncompromising exposition of the dharma. I guess that most were attracted by the first public appearance of a Tibetan lama in Manchester. Some came from the existing Buddhist groups, and quite a few I recognised from earlier years.

The following day, Kalu Rinpoche gave Refuge, followed by the initiation of the deity Chenrezi, embodiment of enlightened compassion, from Mingyur Dorje's collection, to about a dozen people. Only one or two of those who attended this initiation in my apartment in Didsbury still practise dharma today, yet it was the beginning of Vajrayana in Manchester.

After completing this short programme of teaching, Kalu Rinpoche urged me to establish a centre for him in our city. A little surprisingly, he did not refer to any role for Chime Rinpoche. His wish was that it be named Kagyu Ling Tashi Dzong, with the core of its programme being systematic contemplation of the *four thoughts* and the sadhana of Chenrezi composed by the celebrated fifteenth-century yogin Tangtong Gyalpo. As with all Vajrayana sadhanas, this practice is the means by which one gives rise to the enlightened qualities, embodied by the deity, through visualisation and recitation of the deity's liturgy and mantra.

With these injunctions in mind, on the next day I travelled up to Samye Ling in Kalu Rinpoche's entourage. There, I received two further initiations from him: Jatson Nyingpo's initiation of Padmasambhava in the form of Konchok Chindu ('The Union of Jewels') and the initiation of Green Tara from the *Profound Drop* cycle of the nineteenth-century 'treasure revealer', Chogyur Dechen Lingpa. Thus it so happened that my first few initiations belonged to the Nyingma tradition, albeit they were ones that had been assumed into the Kagyu tradition over the years. It was, of course, the Nyingmapa ('The Ancient Ones') who preserved the 'treasures', originally taught and concealed in Tibet by Padmasambhava, the great master from Oddiyana, in the late eighth century and recovered and transmitted by later generations of 'treasure revealers'.

While I was in Samye Ling, Kalu Rinpoche also gave a series of teachings drawn from the Kagyu patriarch Gampopa's famous manual, *Jewel Ornament of Liberation*, which details the graduated practice of the Mahayana path. Privately, he gave me advice on my personal practice, during the course of which he commented on the close links between himself and Karma Thinley

Rinpoche, who, he informed me, was going to lead a centre for him in Toronto.

When I returned from Scotland to start my second year at University, I also began the practice of offering the mandala, the third part of the preliminaries, and the section through which one gathers the 'two accumulations' of spiritual merit and wisdom, essential for progress upon the path. Lacking the proper mandala plates for this practice, items which could not be found outside India in those days, I improvised by using two circular mirrors from Woolworths. It seemed to work. I also organised a weekly meditation on Chenrezi in my apartment, as Kalu Rinpoche had wished. Rather to my surprise, some people who had received the initiation came for a while.

While these small developments were taking place in Manchester, further afield, Samye Ling and Kham House were growing in importance. There were also an increasing number of people interested in Kagyu teachings in London – many of them followers of Chime Rinpoche. These developments led up to the first visit to Britain by H.H. the 16th Gyalwa Karmapa, Rangjung Rigpe Dorje, the fifty-year-old head of the Karma-Kagyu school. It occurred that autumn, as part of his first tour of Europe and North America.

The British segment of his tour began at Samye Ling, where His Holiness Karmapa gave a number of initiations, teachings, and the Vajra Crown ceremony, a famous blessing ritual associated with the line of Karmapas. After visiting Edinburgh, His Holiness and his entourage then travelled southwards, taking in Essex, London, Cambridge and Birmingham, and, although I saw him at these other places, in each of which he performed the Vajra Crown ceremony, it was at Kham

House that I received from him the initiation of the 2nd Karmapa, Karma Pakshi, and that of the goddess Vajra-varahi.

Since this second initiation and its related medita-tion are amongst the most important and esoteric of all Kagyu teachings, attendance was restricted to about twenty of us. This number included Tenga Rinpoche, Ato Rinpoche, Chime Rinpoche, Jigme Rinpoche and Akong Tulku, together with around fifteen Western-ers, including Sister Palmo and her fellow nun, Shen-pen Hookham. Kham House was also the venue for a separate ceremony in which His Holiness gave monastic ordination to a number of people, although it later tran-spired that, in the long term, the American nun Pema Chodron was the only one ordained that day to retain her monastic vows. Before he left there, I was able to have an interview with His Holiness, during which he told me that I should practise the *Four Sessions Guru-Yoga* of the 8th Karmapa, Mikyo Dorje.

During his stay in the U.K., His Holiness made the decision that a Karma-Kagyu institutional structure should be founded. The model he had in mind was that of a charitable organisation, governing all Kagyu activities and groups in the country. Consequently, when His Holiness spent a couple of days in Birmingham, he called a few of us together to announce that he wanted us to establish just such an organisation. The body was to be known as 'The Karma-Kagyu Trust' and was to be under his supreme authority.

Seven of us were appointed as trustees: Ato Rinpoche, Akong Tulku and Chime Rinpoche, two lawyers – John Maxwell, a disciple of Akong Tulku, and Michael Bar-nett, a disciple of Kalu Rinpoche – Michael Hookham (Rikdzin Shikpo), a disciple of Trungpa Rinpoche, and myself, the youngest of the group. His Holiness concluded this initial meeting by bestowing the long-life initiation of Tangtong Gyalpo upon us. Suddenly, at the end of the ritual, a rainbow appeared in the clear blue sky. With such an auspicious sign, all seemed set fair for the new trust.

Yet despite the rainbow, and notwithstanding His Holiness's wishes, difficulties soon emerged. Firstly, Akong Rinpoche revealed that Samye Ling could not belong to the new Trust, as it was already administered by its own charitable body. Then, Chime Rinpoche confirmed that Kham House would also not be incorporated into the Trust. This only left for possible inclusion our fledgling group in Manchester and a small centre in Birmingham, run for that section of the local population of Indian immigrants who had converted to Theravada Buddhism to free themselves from their lowly status within the Hindu social system. The resident monk, Venerable Rewata Dhamma, was an old friend of Sister Palmo from Burma, and it appeared that an unlikely scheme had been devised to bring this centre into the Karma-Kagyu Trust.

In discussing the nascent Kagyu centre in Manchester, His Holiness ignored the prior involvement of both Kalu Rinpoche and Chime Rinpoche, effectively discounting their involvement with the project. While these two omissions were a little perplexing and would have some consequences, I did not think too much about them. I still had a lot to learn.

Shortly before H.H. Karmapa left the country, I had a dream of wandering lost across a desolate moorland. As I was deciding on which route to take, a wild-looking man with blue skin suddenly appeared. Like a father, he took hold of my hand and led me to safety. On awakening, I realised that this must have been Karmapa himself. He had manifested in a form similar to his appearance as

Heruka in Mikyo Dorje's guru-yoga, the very liturgy that he had advised me to practise.

Once this four-month whirlwind that had begun with Kalu Rinpoche's visit had subsided, I wrote to Karma Thinley Rinpoche in Toronto, bringing him up to date with the details concerning the proposed centre for Manchester. His response made the situation even more complex. As I was his student, Rinpoche expressed his wish that the new centre should be the sister-centre of Kampo Gangra Drubgyud Ling, which he had recently established in Toronto in obedience to H.H. Karmapa's command to start centres throughout the world. To this end, he wanted its name to be Kampo Gangra Phuntsok Ling.

This letter put me in a tricky position, but I felt that by working for Rinpoche I would surely also fulfil the injunctions of H.H. Karmapa and Kalu Rinpoche, as, after all, they were his own masters. So it was settled. As a symbol of the centre's complex birth, I suggested to Rinpoche that the Manchester centre should be called Kampo Gangra Kagyu Ling, thus combining the name Rinpoche had been given by H.H. Karmapa with that bestowed by Kalu Rinpoche. Initially, I also tried to retain an acknowledgement of Kalu Rinpoche and Chime Rinpoche in the publicity. However, henceforth, Kagyu Ling was, to all intents and purposes, Karma Thinley Rinpoche's centre.

In fact, within a couple of years, Rinpoche would insist that his centres in both Manchester and Toronto should withdraw from the wider Karma-Kagyu legal structures in their respective countries, while of course continuing to respect H.H. Karmapa as the supreme head of the tradition. It was also at about this same point in time that Kalu Rinpoche would come to the decision that any Western centres founded by him would operate under his sole spiritual authority. In that case, it resulted in his centres being dedicated to the Shangpa Kagyu tradition as well as the Karma-Kagyu.

In all this complexity, I did not lose sight of the fact that my masters were each acting in accord with the bodhisattva imperative to benefit beings, but I did not immediately grasp just how free-wheeling Tibetan lamas are. In other words, although bonds of devotion, established through receiving initiations and other teachings, and clan-based loyalties both have a strong influence in Tibetan religious life, each important lama and his establishment tend to operate quasi-independently, even within the school to which he has a primary connection. However, I had decided to trust Rinpoche's judgement about these matters.

My naïveté in those days probably owed something to my memories of Catholicism's more centralised structures. Now, I had stumbled upon the subterranean politics of the dharma world, where nothing could be addressed too openly but where following one master's wishes could cause you to step on another one's toes, and where any pride at being involved was likely to throw you off balance. It was a sticky situation for a while – probably stickier than I realised at the time. As far as that goes, it took me a few years to understand that, when it comes to negativity, Shantideva gets it right:

> What is there to gain and what is there to lose
> With things which are, in this way, empty?
> Who exists to respect me
> Or to criticise me?

Three months later, Kalu Rinpoche passed through Britain again, on his return to India from the United States. Coincidentally, with some financial assistance, we had just purchased a place for Kagyu Ling in South Manchester, and, fortunately for us, Kalu Rinpoche was happy to perform the consecration-ceremony and also bestow the initiation of Green Tara. Privately, he gave me teachings on guru-yoga, the final part of the preliminaries, in which, through one-pointed devotional practice, one receives the blessings of the lineage and thus can enter into the core practice of *Mahamudra* itself. Nothing further was said by him about the governance of the centre, although his nephew and business manager, Gyaltsen, made a point of asserting to me that Karma Thinley Rinpoche was running the centre in Toronto for Kalu Rinpoche. I listened, but didn't say anything in response.

It was a month after Kalu Rinpoche's visit that a small group of us moved into the new centre, a family-size house in Chorlton, an area popular with both students and young professionals. I asked Angela Brady, a student of Hispanic Studies at the University, to act as a secretary, and some small-scale publicity for the centre was organised. Although none of the rooms in the house were particularly large, the one we adapted as a shrine-room could accommodate the regular meditation on Chenrezi.

There wasn't much of a blue-print for places like ours or Rinpoche's other centre in Toronto, or, indeed, any of the Tibetan Buddhist institutions that sprang up in the West in those years. The paradigmatic Buddhist organisational model has always been monastic, and these Western centres were almost exclusively lay. It is true, of course, that in Eastern Tibet there had been semi-organized communities of non-celibate tantrikas, but that was still rather different from these newly-formed

Western groups, whose members required an education in the basic elements of dharma. Eventually, it would prove possible to formulate such a syllabus, but it would take time. In the event, the simple structure of practice and introductory classes that Rinpoche suggested was similar to that advocated by Kalu Rinpoche for his own expanding community of centres in Europe and North America.

By July of that year, I had completed two years of my undergraduate course in the university, and, more importantly, had finished the guru-yoga and thus the entire set of preliminaries. With the preliminaries completed, I was ready to begin to practise the basic Vajravarahi sadhana that usually follows in the Kagyu tradition, and for which I had already received the requisite initiation from H.H Karmapa. As this cycle of practice is derived from the Chakrasamvara tantra, it belongs to the anuttara-tantra class, the highest of the four sets of tantras. Kagyu practitioners customarily perform the practice of the 'development-stage' of this goddess, through which one's distorted perception of the world is transformed into pure vision, in tandem with formless *Mahamudra* meditation.

It was also at this time that I began to get to know Ato Rinpoche, a friend of Karma Thinley Rinpoche, now living in Cambridge with his English wife, Alathea, a Classicist and friend of Freda Bedi. As a disciple of such eminent masters as Dilgo Khyentse Rinpoche and H.H. Karmapa, Ato Rinpoche had been one of the last generation of lamas to be fully trained in Tibet. He had a courteous, aristocratic presence and enjoyed a considerable reputation amongst Tibetans for his mastery of Vajravarahi and *Mahamudra*. However, it appeared that Ato Rinpoche had no wish to found centres in the West himself. He certainly gave us much help at that time, as a type of 'kindly uncle' figure, visiting Manchester on three occasions, while I travelled to Cambridge numerous times.

During the three-year period from 1975 onwards, he bestowed on me transmissions for such Kagyu and Nyingma works as Karmapa Wangchuk Dorje's *Mahamudra Clearing the Clouds of Unawareness*, *Eight Doha Songs* of Shabaripa and other siddhas, Longchen Rabjam's *Trilogy of Natural Liberation*, *Precious Jewel Ship*, and *Jewel Treasury of Dharmadhatu*, Terton Karma Lingpa's *Liberation by Hearing in the Bardo*, various short works by Rikdzin Jigme Lingpa, Mipham Rinpoche's *Summary of the Gateway to Knowledge*, Jamgon Kongtrul's commentary on the *Seven Points of Mind-Training*, the *Four Dharmas of Gampopa*, and, from the Sakya tradition, the cycle of *Parting from the Four Attachments* and Sakya Pandita's *Treasury of Good Sayings*.

Thanks to Ato Rinpoche, in the summer of 1975, I began the practice of Shamar Chokyi Wangchuk's sadhana of Vajravarahi. As I had already obtained the initiation, it was only necessary for him to give me the relevant reading-transmission and instruction for the daily sadhana, which is itself extracted from a more elaborate form of the practice. At the same time, he gave me the reading-transmissions for the sadhanas of Karma Pakshi and Sangye Menla, the guru-yoga of Karmapa entitled the *Seeds of the Four Kayas* and the guru-yoga of Padmasambhava, known as *Shower of Blessings*, composed by Mipham Rinpoche, which last liturgy later became a firm fixture in all our centres.

My connection with Ato Rinpoche was important in another way also, in that it gave me the chance to receive some teaching from his uncle, Dilgo Khyentse Rinpoche, one of the greatest recent teachers in the Nyingma tradition. Khyentse Rinpoche was renowned for his mastery of the Great Perfection, a system which in Nyingma occupies a position analogous to that of *Mahamudra* in Kagyu.

When Khyentse Rinpoche arrived on tour in England at the beginning of February 1976, he stayed at first in Kham House with Chime Rinpoche, who was also one of his nephews. Unusually tall for a Tibetan, Khyentse Rinpoche was very striking in appearance, with a face full of a compassionate brilliance. He bestowed upon us Chogyur Dechen Lingpa's Secret Drop Vajrakilaya initiation and the reading-transmissions for Patrul Rinpoche's commentary on *Hitting the Essence in Three Words*, a celebrated text containing the three essential instructions of Garab Dorje on the Great Perfection, and Nuden Dorje's *Biography of Yeshe Tsogyal,* the Tibetan consort of Padmasambhava.

When these teachings were finished, Khyentse Rinpoche stayed for some days with Ato Rinpoche in nearby Cambridge, where I was able to spend some private time around him. Since I had completed the *Mahamudra* preliminaries, Khyentse Rinpoche gave me some brief instructions on the Great Perfection system, through which one can achieve Buddhahood by directly recognising that all phenomena, whether arising as cyclic existence (samsara) or nirvana, are primordially pure in their emptiness and therefore 'perfect' as they are.

At that point, there were already plans for Khyentse Rinpoche to travel to Samye Ling and so, with the encouragement of Ato Rinpoche and Karma Thinley Rinpoche, I invited him to spend a couple of days with us in Manchester. Several days later, Khyentse Rinpoche and his party, which included his grandson, Shechen Rabjam Rinpoche, and Tulku Pema Wangyal as his

translator, came to Kagyu Ling. There he gave Refuge
to a few people, and, the next day, bestowed Chogyur
Dechen Lingpa's initiation of the *Heart Accomplishment
which Clears All Obstacles*, a cycle of practice focussing
upon Padmasambhava. He also bestowed the reading-
transmissions for a sadhana of Vajrasattva, likewise from
the 'treasures' of Chogyur Lingpa, for *The Excellent Path
to Enlightenment*, a short text of the preliminaries composed by his predecessor, Jamyang Khyentse Wangpo,
and, finally, for the sadhana of Karma Pakshi, as H.H.
Karmapa had requested him to do. The next day, Khyentse Rinpoche gave Rikdzin Shikpo and myself some
detailed oral teaching on *Hitting the Essence in Three
Words.*

Throughout this time, in a parallel life, I had of
course been attending my University classes. There
was not really a big clash between these different lives,
as my time as an undergraduate was quite supportive
for dharma-studies and practice. At least it afforded
me sufficient time every day to accomplish two major
sessions of practice: one in the early morning and a
second in the evening, as well as periods of retreat in the
vacations. This is a pattern which has continued to serve
me in good stead throughout my life.

As regards my academic studies themselves, the first
two years of my studies at University were dedicated to
Theology, Ecclesiastical History, Biblical Studies and
Comparative Religion. Alongside these, I studied Pali,
the canonical language of the Theravada school, since
one of my lecturers, Mr. Lance Cousins, was a leading
expert in that field. It was only in the second half of my
undergraduate studies that I was able to dedicate myself
exclusively to Comparative Religion and the study of
non-Christian systems. The University of Manchester
had actually been the first University to endow a chair

in Comparative Religion, when they appointed the distinguished Pali scholar, T. W. Rhys Davids, to this position in 1902. So it was undoubtedly one of the best places for such studies.

Outside of the lecture hall, student life still bore some of the marks of the late 1960s. One of these marks was a certain interest in spiritual ideas and practices. The University Buddhist Society, which I had joined four years earlier, was still flourishing, while another group that had achieved a measure of popularity was the Society for the Common Life. This organisation, led by the Welsh spiritual teacher Glyn Davies, was based upon the mystical doctrines of the Cabbala, albeit transposed from their traditional Jewish setting.

In July 1976, I graduated with a B.A. Honours, and was awarded a scholarship by the Department of Education and Science to enable me to study for an M.A. in Comparative Religion. Only a year later, my M.A. work was converted to research for a Ph.D., under the supervision of Professor Trevor Ling and Mr Cousins, both distinguished scholars in the field of Buddhist Studies, although it was actually Karma Thinley Rinpoche's suggestion that my Ph.D. topic should be the history and teachings of the Dakpo-Kagyu tradition in India and Tibet. Unfortunately, my various responsibilities obstructed rapid progress with this work, but I could, at least, improve my rudimentary knowledge of classical Tibetan language a little.

One early contribution to my post-graduate work was provided, fortuitously, by the visit to Kagyu Ling of the Drukpa Kagyu master, the 8th Khamtrul Rinpoche, Dongyud Nyima, in February 1977. He was able to spend a couple of days with us, on his way to Samye Ling, and gave the transmissions of *Liberation by Hearing in the Bardo* and the *Tantra of the Lotus Essence*, both from the 'treasures' of Chogyur Dechen Lingpa. During his stay, I also received from him the reading-transmission for the trilogy of 'Doha songs', composed in mediaeval India by the siddha Saraha, and Tilopa's *Ganges Mahamudra*, both source-texts for the entire Kagyu transmission of *Mahamudra*, and works which I would have to use in my doctoral research.

In the break-time between these transmissions, Khamtrul Rinpoche recounted stories of the visits paid to him by various groups of Indian yogins, in the several years since he and his community of Drukpa refugees had established their community, known as Tashi Jong, close to Dharamsala in Himachal Pradesh. Although, in appearance, these yogins could have been generic Hindu yogins, they identified themselves as Buddhists and revealed that they had preserved lineages of Chakrasamvara practice. It seems that they had been able to survive the dissolution of institutional Indian Buddhism in the late mediaeval period because, as Vajrayana yogins, their external appearance was somewhat similar to the familiar Hindu sadhus, whereas monastic robes would have made them immediately identifiable as 'Buddhist'. I would hear stories about similar encounters from quite a few lamas over the years.

If one had assessed the situation at this point, early in 1977, one might have declared that Vajrayana Buddhism was beginning to be planted successfully in the West. New groups were springing up, with the Gelug and Nyingma traditions following on the heels of the various established Kagyu centres. Perhaps most importantly, H.H. Karmapa now had a seat in the West – Dhagpo Kagyu Ling in the Dordogne region of France – which he had placed under the direction of his nephew, Jigme Rinpoche, the elder brother of Shamar Rinpoche.

Closer to home, Kagyu Ling had now been existent in Manchester for two years, during which time it had been visited by three or four of the most respected masters in the Tibetan world. So you could say that something had started. We would see where it led.

Chapter Two
Banner of Victory

It was early in the morning of the first day of May that Karma Thinley Rinpoche arrived at Manchester Airport on an Air Canada flight from Toronto. It had been four years since I had taken refuge and started on the path. In that time, I had met a few different teachers and made some progress. Now, I would resume my studies with Rinpoche and he would put his stamp on Kagyu Ling, confirming unmistakably that it was his project.

Up until that point, my own training had been mainly contemplative, but, from this time onwards, Rinpoche and other masters would also share textual and philosophical teachings with me. It is such studies that supply the detailed knowledge and analytical skills necessary to sustain a life-time's dharma-practice.

This second visit of Rinpoche to Britain would last a month and commenced with an extensive teaching in Kagyu Ling on the great philosopher Nagarjuna's *Letter to a Friend*. To elucidate the text, he utilised the commentary composed by the fifteenth-century Sakya master, Jetsun Rendawa. On completing this, Rinpoche bestowed Refuge on those who had not previously received it and gave the Bodhisattva Vow from the lineage of Manjushri, the same one that I had received from Chime Rinpoche. This particular version of the core Mahayana commitment had been transmitted by the seventh-century Indian master, Shantideva, in his *Entering the Path of a Bodhisattva*. Shantideva, like Nagarjuna, belonged to the Madhyamaka school of tenets and, consequently, this version of the Bodhisattva Vow is associated with that philosophical school.

The next phase of Rinpoche's programme was concerned specifically with Vajrayana. To begin, he bestowed the initiation of Amitabha from the lineage of Mingyur Dorje, an initiation which Kalu Rinpoche had already bestowed three years previously, and, privately, he gave me the reading-transmission for the entire related set of texts. In the evenings, we worked together on translating this material. Some time later, after Rinpoche had left, I made a fourteen-day retreat on the Amitabha sadhana cycle and a seven-day retreat on the related practice of 'transference' (in Tibetan, *phowa*), which establishes a basis for rebirth in the Buddha-field of Sukhavati at the time of death.

The second initiation given to our members by Rinpoche was that of Konchok Chindu from the lineage of the sixteenth-century 'treasure-revealer', Rikdzin Jatson Nyingpo, whose teachings have spread widely in both Nyingma and Kagyu traditions. As with Amitabha, I had received it previously from Kalu Rinpoche, but from now on I would adopt this as one of my main practices, accomplishing its preliminaries and basic retreat as detailed in Rikdzin Tsewang Norbu's commentary, the transmission for which Rinpoche also gave me. Years later, I would receive this initiation from Rinpoche on two further occasions. I would also obtain the transmission of Jamgon Kongtrul's commentary on the completion-stage of the cycle from Bokar Rinpoche.

Rinpoche shared more treasures of the Kagyu tradition during his stay by bestowing the reading-transmissions of two key works: Gampopa's *Jewel Ornament of Liberation* and Jamgon Kongtrul's *Torch of Certainty*. Then, privately, he gave me a number of other transmissions, including Atisha's *Lamp of the Path of Enlightenment* and *Jewel Rosary of a Bodhisattva*, Tokme Zangpo's *Thirty-Seven Practices of a Buddha's Child*, Geshe Chekhawa's *Seven Points of Mind-Training*, Drakpa Gyaltsen's *Commentary on the King of Aspiration Prayers* and texts by Ngorchen Kunga Zangpo, Jetsun Drakpa Gyaltsen and Sakya Pandita on *Parting from the Four Attachments*.

The presence of quite a few Kadampa texts in this list demonstrates Rinpoche's considerable fondness for that tradition. In fact, he told me that, shortly after his arrival in Canada, he had dreamed of Atisha, the eleventh-century Bengali master, from whose teachings the tradition had sprung. Rinpoche interpreted this as a sign that Kadam dharma would be particularly important for the West. In his youth, Rinpoche had received many Kadam transmissions from his Sakya and Kagyu masters, as well as from Trijang Rinpoche and Ling Rinpoche from the Gelug school. He had also made a pilgrimage to Reting, the first Kadam monastery which was established by Atisha's disciple, Dromton, in 1060.

In addition to these textual transmissions, Rinpoche gave me the transmission of the *Four Sessions Guru-Yoga* composed by Karmapa Mikyo Dorje, which H.H.

Karmapa had already urged me to practise. Rinpoche had himself received this, together with Karma Chakme's written notes for the practice, from the late Khandro Chenmo, the disciple and consort of the 15th Karmapa, Khachab Dorje.

During this month, Rinpoche also made three short trips: one to Samye Ling, one to see his old friend, Ato Rinpoche, in Cambridge, and one to West Wales, where we spent two enjoyable days, close to the coast. We had been invited there by some people who had moved out to the Celtic fringe to set up an alternative community and imagined that Buddhism could play a part in this. It took a few years for this fantasy to wear off.

On the morning of our departure from Pembrokeshire, Rinpoche handed me a sheet of paper. On this, he had written the names for the Kagyu and Sakya centres which he wished me to establish in Britain. Later, on his return to Canada, Rinpoche sent me a handwritten scroll, bearing his formal appointment of me as his representative (in Tibetan, *ku-tshab*). It declared that it was my duty 'to raise the low-flying victory-banner of dharma'. I suppose Rinpoche believed that I could achieve something for him in this role.

After Rinpoche's departure, the autumn of 1977 was a crowded one. In November, I married Jennifer Bavin, a graduate in Philosophy from the University of Manchester. I found out many years later that she had been in two minds about making such a commitment. I must have been too busy to notice that at the time.

Later that same eventful month, thanks to the effort of the Bristol-based musician and artist Steve Mulligan, we started a small Sakya dharma group in that city, in accord with Rinpoche's wishes. It was not a city I knew, but I would have many years to remedy this ignorance. As Steve set about establishing the group, he was aided by number of people, particularly two indomitable young women, Jean Vesey and Sylvia Lerner.

Within weeks, H.H. Karmapa returned for a second visit to Britain. On this occasion, Kagyu Ling hosted him in Manchester. The venue that we used for his teachings was a church hall in the suburb of Fallowfield, a few miles south of the city centre. Nowadays this church hall is a bar, popular with the drinking classes. Sic transit gloria mundi!

His Holiness performed the Vajra Crown ceremony, and subsequently gave the initiations of two lineage masters, Milarepa and Karma Pakshi, to members of Kagyu Ling and other Buddhists. At the request of Lance Cousins, I also arranged for His Holiness to give the initiation of Sangye Menla, the 'Medicine Buddha', in the Samatha Centre, a local Theravada institute. This took place shortly before His Holiness departed Manchester.

His Holiness's entourage included Jamgon Kongtrul Rinpoche, the third in his series of incarnations, who taught *The Four Dharmas of Gampopa* while with us. In private, Kongtrul Rinpoche gave me the reading-transmissions for the rituals of the Protectors, Mahakala Dorje Bernagchen and Six-Armed Mahakala. Also present in His Holiness's party was the yogin and scholar Khenpo Tsultrim Gyamtso, an old friend of Karma Thinley Rinpoche from Nangchen.

After H.H. Karmapa's departure from Britain, Khenpo Tsultrim stayed in the country for a little while, and I visited him in London to receive the reading-transmission of the *Supreme Continuity*, Maitreya's treatise on the Buddha-nature. Although Maitreya's text has been interpreted in a number of ways since its appearance in the fourth century, Khenpo Tsultrim himself espoused the Zhentong (Extrinsic Emptiness) perspective, and thus presented the work from the standpoint of that variant line of Madhyamaka philosophy.

In a sense, this transmission actually marked the beginning of my studies of that particular view. It was a system of thought popularised by such fourteenth-century Tibetan thinkers as Dolpopa Sherab Gyaltsen and Karmapa Rangjung Dorje, and was quite distinct from the more normative Madhyamaka followed by most masters in India and Tibet, whether Svatantrika or Prasangika. Early in the next decade, I would receive more extensive teachings on this system from Karma Thinley Rinpoche himself.

Not long afterwards, I received some further instructions on Great Perfection meditation, when H.H. Dudjom Rinpoche, the erudite head of the Nyingma, visited London. It was the second time that I had seen him, having received some teachings some two years before. On this occasion, I also received the initiations of Dorje Drolo, Hayagriva and Vajrakilaya from his 'treasure' lineage.

Alongside acquiring such teachings, my responsibilities increased a little that summer, when Karma Thinley Rinpoche sent me the authority to bestow Refuge. Perhaps mindful that it would be a year or so before he himself could visit again, Rinpoche included a list of male and female religious names for those who requested the ceremony. In the same letter, he informed me that he had invited H.H. Sakya Trizin to visit our recently established group, Sakya Thinley Rinchen Ling in Bristol. Rinpoche had actually named the group in honour of His Holiness's grandfather, Dakshul Thinley Rinchen, the 39th Sakya Trizin, and the master who had recognised Rinpoche as a Sakya incarnation. In the event, it turned out that this visit would have major consequences for me.

Four years had passed since I had met His Holiness in London and five years since taking refuge with Karma Thinley Rinpoche. During that time, my studies and practice had been largely a mixture of Kagyu and Nyingma teachings; my studies in the Sakya tradition had been confined to the cycle of *Parting from the Four Attachments,* a series of Mahayana *Mind-Training* teachings, originating in Sachen Kunga Nyingpo's vision of the Bodhisattva Manjushri in 1104. However, over the next several years, this limited knowledge would be replaced by a wider understanding of Sakya teaching and its unique qualities. At the same time, I would also begin to discover the complexities involved in serving two traditions in fulfilment of Rinpoche's two-fold loyalties.

It was in August that H.H. Sakya Trizin arrived in Britain. Initially, he stayed at Chime Rinpoche's centre in Essex, where I visited him to renew our invitation and to receive the initiation of Vajrasattva derived from the Guhyasamaja Tantra. A few days later, His Holiness, together with his wife, Dagmo Kushog-la, his three-year-old son, Ratna Vajra Rinpoche, and three attendants, came to stay with us in Bristol. We spent a week in a pleasant garden apartment, lent to us by two artists. It was situated in the Clifton district of the city, close by the famous Suspension Bridge built by Brunel in the nineteenth century.

His Holiness was unstintingly generous during his time with us. His programme of teachings included four initiations, those of Manjushri Sakya Pandita and Chenrezi-Mahamudra, in addition to Vajravarahi and Mahakala from Bari Lotsava's collection of sadhanas.

Following these, His Holiness gave two days of comprehensive teachings on *The Three Visions*, utilising the text of the sixteenth-century master, Ngawang Chodrak.

This set of instructions represents the first part of the *Path and its Fruit*, the principal teaching of the Sakya school, and a system of practice issuing from the Indian siddha Virupa's understanding of the Hevajra Tantra cycle. However, as a preliminary teaching, *The Three Visions* – the 'impure', 'experiential' and 'pure' visions – utilises the non-tantric teachings common to all vehicles. Dharma students came from many different parts of the country to be present at this major event.

To conclude his teaching, His Holiness gave the meditation-transmission of Tangtong Gyalpo's famous sadhana of Chenrezik. As there was also some free time during these days, I was able to obtain instructions from His Holiness for the preliminaries specific to *The Three Tantras*, the exclusively tantric part of the *Path and its Fruit*.

As a result of this time with His Holiness, I felt a great confidence in his tradition. It was as if the seeds of the Sakya teachings, planted both by Rinpoche at Refuge and by my previous meeting with His Holiness himself, had now been activated. It became plain to me that, from now on, His Holiness would be one of my main lamas. Consequently, on his departure, I began to practise the Sakya Pandita guru-yoga, something that Rinpoche had advised me would attract the blessings of the sages of the Sakya tradition.

Happily enough, our daughter Rosalind was born just a few weeks after His Holiness and his family left, and that same month Karma Thinley Rinpoche briefly passed through England on his way to India. It was Rinpoche's first trip there since leaving for Canada in 1971, and his intention was to receive the *Treasury of Pre-*

cious Revealed Teachings, Jamgon Kongtrul's monumental compilation of Nyingma systems of practice, from Dilgo Khyentse Rinpoche. During this stop-over in London, we were able to make plans for the programme of teachings that he would deliver in Britain the following summer.

Before that planned visit could happen in 1979, however, we enjoyed visits from three other masters – Chime Rikdzin Rinpoche, Phende Rinpoche and Gendun Rinpoche – each of whom embodied a slightly different side of the dharma. The first of these was the Nyingma lama, Chime Rikdzin Rinpoche, a holder of the Dorje Drak line of 'treasures', who toured Britain in January, accompanied by his daughter Lakshmi, and long-term student James Low, now a well-respected teacher in his own right. 'C.R. Lama', as Chime Rikdzin Rinpoche was often known, was a somewhat colourful but accomplished master, who, after leaving Tibet at the beginning of the 1950s, had become a University professor at Shantiniketan, the school of studies founded in Bengal by the Nobel laureate, Rabindranath Tagore. He was a lama who was not afraid to voice fairly vigorous views, capable of ruffling feathers, whether Western or Tibetan.

At my invitation, Chime Rikdzin Rinpoche visited Bristol, where, in between subjecting those attending to a dharma-interrogation, he gave some teachings on *The Three Visions.* Kagyu Ling was his second venue, where he bestowed the initiation of the *Assembly of Vidyadharas,* the inner 'sadhana of the guru' from the Longchen Nyingtik cycle, the famous collection of teachings revealed by the eighteenth-century master, Rikdzin Jigme Lingpa. For some time, I had wanted to receive this initiation to extend my knowledge of this cycle, some elements of which I had already received from Ato Rinpoche. While he was with us, Chime Rikdzin Rinpoche also gave me a number of reading-transmissions from that collection and found the time for Mipham Rinpoche's *Precious Lamp of Certainty*, a work which greatly influenced my understanding of Madhyamaka and how it can be harmonised with Vajrayana.

Shortly after this visit, I established a connection with Phende Shabdrung Rinpoche, Jamyang Kunzang Chokyi Gyamtso, an important lama in the Ngor tradition of Sakya and disciple of three great masters – Ngawang Lekpa, Phende Khen Rinpoche and Dampa Rinpoche – with whom he had trained in Tibet. Having left India in the late 1960s, Rinpoche had initially spent some time at Samye Ling and in Cambridge with Ato Rinpoche. Together with his French wife, Jamyang Khandro, and their three children, he had then finally settled in Normandy. There, close to the town of Evreux, they had established a centre, named Ewam Phende Ling.

Karma Thinley Rinpoche had known Phende Rinpoche in India, and so now, with Rinpoche's blessings, I invited him to Bristol in the February of that year. He arrived with Jamyang Khandro as his translator and his brother Thubten as his assistant. In fact, although he knew a little English from his years in India, Phende Rinpoche had not mastered French at all, but his teaching was certainly full of the dignity and richness of the Sakya tradition in general and of the Ngorpa subline in particular.

This first visit of his was fairly brief, with two initiations: the initiation of the Lords of the Three Families (the three bodhisattvas: Manjushri, Chenrezi and Vajrapani) and the initiation of Amitayus and Hayagriva from the lineage of Tangtong Gyalpo. Privately, he gave me the transmission of various Sakya liturgies such as the ritual of the Sixteen Arhats, the Praises of the Five Venerable Masters, the guru-yoga of Ngorchen Kunga Zangpo, founder of the Ngorpa tradition, and the ritual of the Dharma Protectors, composed by his own master, Ngawang Lekpa.

This visit was followed by one paid to Kagyu Ling by the *Mahamudra* meditation-master Gendun Rinpoche, from the Nangchen province of Eastern Tibet, whom H.H. Karmapa had installed at the newly-established Dhagpo Kagyu Ling. Lama Gendun visited Britain from France in the spring of 1979, together with Lama Garwang, a Kagyu lama later resident in Holland. In all, he spent five days with us, giving two initiations from Chogyur Lingpa's lineage – the Secret Drop Vajrakilaya and the Profound Drop Tara – as well as the initiations of Akshobya from the tradition of Atisha and White Manjushri from the tradition of Mati Panchen.

During these days, Lama Garwang bestowed the transmission of Rikdzin Jigme Lingpa's *Instruction of the Wisdom Guru* on Gendun Rinpoche and myself. This renowned text is one of the most complete presentations of the practices of the *Innermost Essence* cycle of the Great Perfection and has proved enormously influential, since its appearance in the mid-eighteenth century. I had asked Gendun Rinpoche for this, but, as he had not received it himself, Lama Garwang volunteered to give the transmission, which he had obtained many years previously from Kalu Rinpoche. Gendun Rinpoche and I sat upon the floor while Lama Garwang read the transmission.

That same February, I was appointed to the post of lecturer in the History of Ideas in Manchester Polytechnic (later renamed Manchester Metropolitan University). My lecturing duties in this position were not particularly adjacent to my academic field, but our financial situation, especially now with a child, made it a necessity for me to accept this work. I could continue with my Ph.D. research at the University of Manchester, alongside preparing material for my new lecture courses, the first being *The Rise of Secularism: from The Reformation to the French Revolution* and the second, *Ideas in Contemporary Life: from Marx to Psychoanalysis*. Amusingly enough, since I had no training in academic Philosophy or the political sciences, I was forced to draw upon my studies in Theology and Ecclesiastical History for some of this material – material which I had thought that I had permanently escaped. I must have needed to learn that, sometimes, the past wasn't far behind. Works by scholars like Norman Cohn, Roger Scruton, Jacob Burckhardt and Christopher Lasch came in pretty useful, too.

In actuality, although it might seem distant from dharma, working in this field helped me to understand the importance of acknowledging our native culture. Without such acknowledgement, Buddhism cannot be transplanted effectively, since an acculturated, rootless people can neither be appropriate recipients nor effective agents of its onward transmission. It was transplanted successfully in Asian countries when elements that were valuable in the existing cultural matrix were refined through contact with the trans-historical and trans-cultural truths of the dharma. Of course, this creative use of elements in our cultural environment that are supportive of dharma should not be confused with compromising its essential truths by creating hybrids, whether it be Christianity-and-Buddhism or Materialism-and-Buddhism, or some other such invention. Such intrinsically contradictory mixed-up confusion would have no power to liberate from delusion, the very root of suffering.

A year later, the University of Manchester, my alma mater, would also employ me to teach courses on Mahayana Buddhism and Tibetan Religion for their undergraduate and post-graduate programmes. Until the end of my University work over twenty years later, my academic teaching would be divided between these two institutions and these two fields – Buddhist Studies and recent Western intellectual history.

Poetry is perhaps one such space where some elements of our cultural inheritance might resonate with dharma. It is somehow appropriate, therefore, that during his two summers teaching at Naropa Institute, Chogyam Trungpa Rinpoche's school in Colorado, Karma Thinley Rinpoche came to know some of the American poets who had become Trungpa Rinpoche's followers. Among these were Allen Ginsberg and Anne Waldman, author of 'Fast Speaking Woman'. A couple of years later, I met Anne, and at that time we arranged two poetry readings as fund-raisers for our groups in Bristol and Manchester. The readings happened that June 1979, when Anne, together with Allen Ginsberg and Peter Orlovsky, returned to England.

To hear some of the very poems – like Kaddish and Howl – that had spoken to me so strongly years before was like the closing of a circle. However, I felt that Allen's later, more 'Buddhist' poetry, which he also read at these events, lacked the power that had been present in such early works. It was too didactic – the kind of poetry that Keats would describe as 'having a palpable design upon you'. Allen told me that he and Karma Thinley Rinpoche had composed a spontaneous poem together at Naropa. Rinpoche had certainly kept very quiet about that.

A month later, Rinpoche himself arrived from India. Although even he did not realise it at the time, he had contracted tuberculosis while attending Khyentse Rinpoche's teachings in the Nyingma settlement at Clement Town, close to Dehra Dun. It would only be diagnosed after his return to Toronto. The first location for his teaching in this country was a farmhouse in Carmarthenshire, where a number of people had gathered for a week of practice. When Rinpoche suddenly sent a message announcing his imminent arrival, I hurried to London Heathrow and brought him back to Wales.

Despite being a little indisposed, Rinpoche gave several days of teaching on the 8th Situ Tenpai Nyingje's commentary for the 3rd Karmapa's *Aspiration Prayer of Mahamudra*. This commentary is simultaneously an elucidation of Karmapa Rangjung Dorje's verses and a defence of the Kagyu vision of how *Mahamudra* is to be understood and practised. Having concluded this major teaching, Rinpoche bestowed the One Thousand-Armed Chenrezi initiation from the lineage of Bhikshuni Lakshminkara. He also gave Refuge to a number of people, including my daughter, Rosalind, to whom he gave the name Karma Sangye Dronma, and her life-long friend, Anna Golding, whom he named Karma Damcho Dronma.

Moving from there to our Sakya group in Bristol, Rinpoche then gave several days of teaching on *Discriminating the Three Vows* by Sakya Pandita – ironically enough, one of the works to which the 8th Situ was implicitly responding in the commentary that Rinpoche had just taught in Wales. In the course of this, Rinpoche mentioned his regret at not having more time to elucidate the commentarial traditions on this polemical text.

Sakya Pandita's work argues that various errors had aris-
en in the Kagyu, Kadam and Nyingma schools in Tibet
which contradict the Indian sources of dharma and the
teachings of their own founding masters. In fact, over
the years, it has exerted a major impact on my understanding of the three vehicles – Shravaka, Bodhisattva
and Vajrayana.

The last few days of Rinpoche's visit were spent in
Kagyu Ling in Manchester, where he taught Geshe
Langri Thangpa's *Eight Verses of Mind-Training* from
the Kadam tradition and gave the initiation of Sangye
Menla from the Sky Dharma treasures. Privately,
Rinpoche bestowed upon me the reading-transmission
for the Vajravarahi mandala ritual composed by the 6th
Karmapa, Thongwa Donden. Then, before leaving, he
instructed me to teach some of the works that he had
bestowed on his previous visit, such as the *Letter to a
Friend*, the *Thirty-Seven Practices*, *Parting from the Four
Attachments* and the *Jewel Ornament of Liberation*.

It was also during his stay that we transferred the legal
ownership of the Kagyu Ling house in Manchester,
which had been held in the name of a sponsor, to
Rinpoche. We had managed to pay off the mortgage of
£6,000, and now took this step to signify Rinpoche's
spiritual authority. Rinpoche accepted this happily and
the transfer was made. However, I'm not sure that he
understood our thinking exactly.

In any event, it would be nine years before Rinpoche
would return to England, during which time I would
travel to Canada four times to receive teachings from
him. Rinpoche's many years away from this country
were just long enough for me to understand that, although the centres were founded under his authority,
he did not see himself as the resident lama here. What
is undeniable, however, is that his absence, combined

with the lingering fall-out from the dharma politics of the years from 1975 onwards, made us less confident in developing our projects than might have been the case otherwise. As a result, we were somewhat distanced from the centre of things, especially in the Kagyu world.

On reflection now, I think that, around this time, Rinpoche was beginning to shift his focus to Asia and away from the West. His hopes to establish a seminary style college of studies in Toronto, which he had named Mikyo Dorje Institute, in honour of the 8th Karmapa, had been dashed after a couple of years. What is worse is that his centre in Florida had been destroyed, and the centre that he had established in New Zealand in 1978 had been given to another lama.

Just before the end of that year came the visit of the Kagyu philosophical master Thrangu Rinpoche. Originally abbot of Thrangu monastery in East Tibet, Thrangu Rinpoche had played an important role in the education of many of the young incarnations of the Karma-Kagyu tradition at Rumtek in Sikkim, the monastic seat in exile of H.H. Karmapa. Now, at the invitation of Akong Tulku, he was making his first tour of Europe. While he was with us, he gave the initiation of Marpa and bestowed upon me the reading-transmissions for Jetsun Milarepa's *Song of the Middle Way View, The Guide to the Karma Pakshi Sadhana*, composed by Karmapa Khachab Dorje, and the gana-puja for this cycle, written by Karmapa Thegchog Dorje, and some teaching on Mipham Rinpoche's *Precious Lamp of Certainty*. In December, following Thrangu Rinpoche's departure, I accomplished the retreat on Marpa guru-yoga, as I had done a year earlier for that of Milarepa.

Chapter Three
Following the Path

In such a way the decade of the 1970s came to an end. The following ten years would have a very different complexion to them. Families, careers and houses might fill the frame entirely during this coming decade, if you weren't really resolved on practice, and some people did disappear that way.

In the world outside dharma, there were discontinuities and continuities. Margaret Thatcher and Ronald Reagan had come to power on the two sides of the Atlantic, and this signalled some temporary shift, economically and politically. However, the cultural forces bred out of Mr Freud and Mr Marx that had been evident on the University campuses of the previous two decades were going to be increasingly significant, as the ambitious and ideologically-driven from my generation began to take up senior positions in education and the media. In the long run, this would prove more influential than any change of personnel in political office.

For Buddhism in the West, the 1980s were, more than anything else, a period of consolidation. Centres had been established, but the first wave of development had now given way to a more sedate rate of growth. This slow-down was an indication that the development of dharma here was going to be more complicated than we had imagined. Spiritual matters had begun to lose the air of fashionability that had attracted some of the young and curious-minded in the previous two decades. A more politically partisan culture was rising in the West, and this culture would only strengthen over the years to come. Its incipient totalitarianism and thirst for an earthly paradise would squeeze or subvert Buddhism, whenever it bumped up against it.

I was certainly not thinking about such matters when, in January 1980, I flew to see Karma Thinley Rinpoche in Toronto. It was my first time on the North American continent, and I was excited to be there to see him and pick up my studies once more. As I stood in the piercing cold on the city's Yonge Street, 'the longest street in North America', I remembered Kerouac's words at the end of *On the Road* about that vast landmass rolling on all the way until the West Coast, and breathed slowly to steady myself.

At that time, Rinpoche was living in a tiny attic-apartment on North Sherborne Street, made available to him by the wealthy husband of one of Chogyam Trungpa's many mistresses. The main part of the house was occupied by Professor A.R.G. Owen, who lectured in Mathematics at the University of Toronto. Outside of the University, Professor Owen conducted research into 'extra-sensory phenomena', and, on one occasion, invited Rinpoche to meet Uri Geller, the famous psychic and spoon bender. Rinpoche, and his cutlery, remained genially unimpressed by this encounter.

It was a little cold up there in the attic, but Rinpoche began an intense three-week period of private teaching by continuing my introduction to the Zhentong system. Although I had received the *Supreme Continuity* two years previously from Khenpo Tsultrim, Rinpoche gave me the reading-transmission for this text again. In subsequent years, Rinpoche would continue with further transmissions of various Zhentong works, particularly those authored by the 3rd Karmapa and Jamgon Kongtrul, and thus I would get to know the subtle points of this system, where the buddha-nature is identified as the ultimately real. This stands in some contrast to the general Madhyamaka view that emptiness, which is characterised as the lack of any abiding nature in phenomena, is to be regarded as the ultimate truth.

According to the Zhentong view, the buddha-nature itself is the unconditioned wisdom-mind, inherent in all beings and hence truly existent. Thus, while Zhentongpa thinkers accept that emptiness characterises all conditioned phenomena, they argue that the buddha-nature itself, being uncreated and therefore unconditioned, cannot be so characterised. The buddha-nature is, in this way, extrinsically empty (in Tibetan, *zhentong*) of anything contingent, but not intrinsically empty (in Tibetan, *rangtong*) of its own primordially enlightened qualities. Those masters who uphold this system claim that it represents the definitive teaching of the Buddha, as set forth both in various Mahayana discourses and in the tantras.

After the *Supreme Continuity*, Rinpoche bestowed upon me the initiation of the great eleventh- to twelfth-century yogini, Machik Labdron, from the lineage of Karma Chakme, together with the related ritual of Chod, composed in the nineteenth century by Jamgon Kongtrul. I had received the Longchen Nyingtik system of Chod ('Severance') from Ato Rinpoche, but this particular version of the practice had been obtained directly from Jamgon Kongtrul by Rinpoche's great uncle, the yogin Jamyang Tenphel. It had thus come to be particularly associated with Rinpoche's Bongsar family. Nowadays, it is a regular part of the programme of rituals at Rinpoche's nunnery in Kathmandu.

To accompany this teaching, Rinpoche gave me the reading-transmissions for Dampa Sangye's *Advice to the People of Dingri* and the *Ladder of Enlightenment* – a small collection of songs by Jamyang Tenphel – both works related, in some way, to the practice of Chod, through which one 'severs' all aspects of self-centredness in the space of emptiness and compassion. Rinpoche emphasised to me that the core of the practice of Chod was the technique of 'opening the door of space', in which one blends one's awareness with the realm of ultimate reality, the Perfection of Wisdom. This is the decisive severance of the 'Mara', or obstructive force, of self-conceit.

Although I had received Ngawang Chodrak's version of the *Three Visions* of the *Path and its Fruit* from H.H. Sakya Trizin two years earlier, Rinpoche bestowed upon me the reading-transmission for Ngorchen Konchok Lhundrub's *Beautiful Ornament of the Three Visions*, the fullest textual presentation of this part of *The Path and its Fruit*. Alongside this, he gave me the transmission of the collection of Sakya daily monastic prayers. Then, Rinpoche proceeded to give me the reading-transmissions for Gampopa's *Precious Rosary of the Supreme Path* and his own *Mirror of Lapis Lazuli*, a condensed verse form of the same master's *Jewel Ornament*.

For some time we had been preparing Rinpoche's *History of the Sixteen Karmapas of Tibet* for publication. I had now edited it and composed some introductory material and notes. Consequently, I spent a little time discussing this work with Rinpoche and two of his Canadian students, Steve Fruitman (Ngakpa Sengge Dorje) and John McCann, both of whom had some involvement in the project. Shambhala's new imprint, Prajna Press, was to bring it out a few months after my visit to Rinpoche. It would sell modestly over the years.

At the end of this first of four trips to Toronto, I had much to study and practise. It seemed that Rinpoche was training me to substitute for him by conferring important transmissions that I would pass on later with his blessing. At the same time, my approach to the dharma was being shaped by Rinpoche's own non-sectarian perspective, a perspective which was made evident in the range of teaching that he would continue to give to me.

Once I was back in England with this collection of teachings to assimilate, it was not long before the second visit of Phende Rinpoche to Bristol. This time he had a slightly more extensive programme. To the members of the centre, he gave the initiation of Green Tara from the lineage of Atisha and the initiation of the main Sakya dharma protector, Gonpo Gur, in the mandala of eight deities. Tara was a deity of especial importance for Phende Rinpoche, her protection having accompanied him in various perilous situations, especially during the escape from Communist Chinese pursuers, as he and his party fled Tibet in 1959.

Following these initiations, he gave me the reading-transmissions for Sakya Pandita's *Elucidating the Thought of the Sage* and Shantideva's *Entering the Path*

of a Bodhisattva, together with its commentary by Lo-
pon Sonam Tsemo. Both these texts were part of the
scholarly curriculum of Sakya, the former work being
a brilliant exposition of the Graduated Path system of
Mahayana. As for Sonam Tsemo's text, it is an extraordinarily detailed commentary on Shantideva's account
of the bodhisattva's journey to Buddhahood, a journey
that begins with the generation of the altruistic attitude
of bodhichitta.

In May, H.H. Karmapa made a fleeting visit to England,
on the way to New York. It would be the last time that
most of us there would see him. Representatives of
dharma-centres from all over Europe gathered, making
it difficult to exchange more than a sentence or two
with him. We did, however, all pass a pleasant afternoon
around him in an impressive house by the Thames,
owned by one of those moneyed enthusiasts who
invariably emerged when a famous master was in town.

Besides Phende Rinpoche, two other Sakya lamas
visited us in Bristol that year. The first to come was
H.H. Sakya Dagchen Rinpoche, head of the Phuntsog
Phodrang branch of the Khon dynasty. Dagchen
Rinpoche, who had been settled with his family in
Seattle for two decades, spent a few days with us, during
which time he gave teachings on the *Four Seals*, followed
by the initiation of Vajrapani Bhutadamara and the
torma initiation of Vajrakilaya.

In private, he gave me the reading-transmissions
for Jetsun Drakpa Gyaltsen's *Path and its Fruit as Given
to Jochak*, Virupa's *Vajra Verses of the Path and its Fruit*,
Sachen's *An Explanation to Aseng* and Jetsun Drakpa
Gyaltsen's *Song of the Inseparability of Samsara and
Nirvana*.

The second of the two Sakya masters to come was Thartse Khen Rinpoche. Like his friend Phende Rinpoche,
Thartse Khen hailed from the Ngor sub-sect of Sakya,
founded in the fifteenth century by Ngorchen Kunga
Zangpo. Khen Rinpoche himself was a distinguished
scholar, having held the throne of Ngor E-wam Choden
for three years in the 1950s as a young lama of the Thartse abbatial house. After going into exile in 1959, at the
age of twenty-six, he had spent fifteen years in Japan,
where he worked on a number of academic projects and
discovered a life far different from his destined career as
a major incarnate lama. As a consequence, he had even
adopted a Japanese name – Hiroshi Sonami – a partial
translation of his Tibetan personal name, Sonam Gyamtso, into Japanese.

For a variety of reasons, things did not work out for him
in Japan, and in 1975 Thartse Khen moved to California
to join his brother, Thartse Shabdrung Rinpoche, who
had established Ewam Choden in Berkeley, one of the
first Sakya centres in North America. It was our good
fortune that he was visiting Europe at that time. While
he was in Bristol, he gave some teachings to students
on Vajrasattva and the rituals of the dharma protectors.
However, he also found the time to give me several days
of teaching on the view of 'the inseparability of samsara
and nirvana', as it is detailed in Konchok Lhundrup's
Three Tantras.

Meanwhile, that autumn, at Kagyu Ling, we hosted
a second visit from Thrangu Rinpoche, who had
returned to bestow the initiations of Gampopa and
White Tara, the practice of the latter being particularly
important for strengthening one's life-force. After these
empowerments, he gave me the reading-transmissions
for all the Indian and Tibetan root texts of *Mahamudra*

and the *Six Doctrines of Naropa* collected by Jamgon Kongtrul in his *Treasury of Spiritual Instructions.*

Besides such visits, I was starting to become busier and gave formal teachings in Manchester, Bristol and elsewhere, as Karma Thinley Rinpoche wished. These included short works such as the *Thirty-Seven Practices*, *Letter to a Friend* and *Parting from the Four Attachments* as well as longer courses on the *Jewel Ornament of Liberation* and *Entering the Path of a Bodhisattva*. Such Mahayana teaching would be my main dharma-work for the rest of that decade.

In January 1981, we were able to invite the famous Great Perfection master, Orgyen Tulku, and one of his sons, Chokyi Nyima Rinpoche, to Kagyu Ling. Orgyen Rinpoche was the principal holder of Chogyur Dechen Lingpa's 'treasure' teachings, and a relative of Karma Thinley Rinpoche. Having trained in Tibet with such masters as Lama Samten Gyamtso, he included numerous great lamas among his own disciples, not least, H.H. Karmapa, to whom he had given the transmission of Chogyur Lingpa's 'Treasures'. Although Orgyen Tulku was not an ordained monastic, H.H. Karmapa had appointed him as the head of a nunnery, Nagi Gompa, just above the Kathmandu Valley, a set of responsibilities which he had embraced unreservedly.

Orgyen Tulku was a perfect example of a master of the Great Perfection – relaxed and easy in his actions – during the few days that he was with us. In this time, he gave teachings on the *Four Dharmas of Gampopa*, together with the pointing-out instructions of the Great Perfection. Following this, Orgyen Tulku gave the initiation of Vajrasattva and the *Heart Accomplishment that Dispels All Obstacles* from Choling's 'treasures' and, in private, bestowed upon me the initiation and reading-transmissions of the *Heart Drop of Samantabhadra*, Chogyur Lingpa's cycle of Peaceful and Wrathful deities practice.

It was only a couple of months later that Kagyu Ling hosted His Eminence the 12th Tai Situ Rinpoche, then making his first visit to the West. Situ Rinpoche was third in the ranking of Karma-Kagyu hierarchy, after H.H. Karmapa and Shamar Rinpoche, the Black and Red Hat Karmapas respectively. He bestowed the initiations of Vajrasattva and Chenrezi, as well as giving four days teaching on Madhyamaka philosophy during his stay.

In May of that same year, Phende Rinpoche came to Bristol to bestow the highly important three-day causal and path initiations of Hevajra, the principal deity of the *Path and its Fruit*. In the course of these initiations, I experienced some of the stated signs and, on the night they concluded, I dreamed that Phende Rinpoche himself knocked on the door of my house to announce that he had delivered a new car for me. On awakening, I felt that I had entered into the stream of blessings of the Sakya tradition. Following the initiation, Phende Rinpoche gave me the reading-transmissions for three Hevajra sadhanas, the *Guru-Yoga of the Profound Path* and *The Guru-Puja of the Path and its Fruit*.

At this same time, Phende Rinpoche, following on from my studies with Thartse Khen, gave me some further teaching on 'the inseparability of samsara and nirvana', the view through which one understands that, while all appearances, whether contaminated or pure, arise from mind, mind itself is not any kind of 'substance' since, when examined, it is found to be empty of any intrinsic nature by which it might be grasped. Nevertheless, as it is taught, one should not conclude that mind is simply non-existent, 'a dead emptiness', since the very manifestation of appearances is due to mind's characteristic luminosity, without which they could not arise. In short, therefore, the essence of mind is simultaneously luminous and empty.

When this point is truly realised through meditation practice, what previously appeared as samsara is realised to be no other than nirvana itself, since it is merely the efflorescence of the luminosity of mind, and this, as already established, cannot be separated from the mind's intrinsic emptiness or nirvanic aspect. Thus, nirvana is not to be won through abandoning samsara, since the latter is merely the former, misperceived.

In the light of this view, it becomes clear that practice of the development stage of an anuttara-tantra deity's sadhana, such as that of Hevajra, is the means to realise the luminous aspect of mind, while the subsequent completion-stage practice enables one to realise the empty aspect of mind. When, subsequently, this luminosity and emptiness are understood to be inseparably united, one has, according to my Sakya masters, acquired the wisdom of Mahamudra.

Finally, Phende Rinpoche gave me the *Fourteen Root Downfalls of Vajrayana* according to the two works of Jetsun Drakpa and Sakya Pandita, extensive and abbreviated respectively. Through these, I learned how one guards against the root and branch downfalls of Vajrayana and thus keeps one's vows intact. Later that year, I visited him in Normandy, where he provided a further postscript to the Hevajra initiation by teaching me the esoteric hatha-yoga practices of the *Path and its Fruit*.

It was only a few days after Phende Rinpoche's significant visit to Bristol that I flew to Toronto to see

Karma Thinley Rinpoche. There, Rinpoche continued the process of my education in *The Path and its Fruit*, when he gave me the reading-transmission of the *Beautiful Ornament of the Three Tantras* by Ngorchen Konchok Lhundrup. This text is the most detailed explanation of the tantric part of the cycle, detailing the three continua (tantra) of basis, path and fruit.

During the same visit, Rinpoche also bestowed the transmission of Jamgon Kongtrul's *Lion's Roar*, an extensive commentary on the *Supreme Continuity*, and the transmission of the *Collected Songs of Spiritual Realisation* composed by his fifteenth-century predecessor, the first Karma Thinleypa, with whom, appropriately enough, he shared a joint Sakya and Kagyu pedigree. Finally, Rinpoche bestowed upon me the reading-transmission of the collection of prayers to Padmasambhava, entitled the *Supplication in Seven Chapters*, one of the essential daily liturgies in Nyingma monasteries. It had originally been revealed as a 'treasure' by Rigdzin Godemchen and arranged as a practice in its present form by Jamyang Khyentse Wangpo in the nineteenth century. Once again, by the end of this visit, Rinpoche had given me a non-sectarian array of teachings.

September saw Thartse Khen Rinpoche visit us for the second time from California. At Kagyu Ling, he gave a course on Chandrakirti's *Entering into the Middle Way* with the commentary composed by Khenpo Zhenga. Chandrakirti's text is the seminal work of Prasangika Madhyamaka philosophy and Khenpo Zhenga, who taught in Sakya and Nyingma monasteries in East Tibet, had been a very distinguished proponent of this system of thought. However, his understanding of it should not be confused with that of Je Tsongkhapa and other Gelug thinkers who also espoused Prasangika, not least since

Khenpo Zhenga had a profound respect for the work of Gorampa Sonam Sengge, famous for his critique of Tsongkhapa's rather idiosyncratic version of the system.

Although Thartse Khen Rinpoche found time to watch the wedding of H.R.H. Prince Charles and Lady Diana Spencer on a television set that we hired at his request, he also gave me further instruction on the *Beautiful Ornament of The Three Tantras,* in particular on the paths associated with the four anuttara initiations. He illustrated this teaching with many tales from his time in Ngor E-wam Choden, as well as from the history of the lineage.

Thartse Khen Rinpoche was one of the most unconventional lamas whom I ever met. His years in Japan and America, combined with his knowledge of different cultures, seemed to have detached him from the usual expectations and assumptions of Tibetan life. To support himself he had taken up pottery in Berkeley, leaving the teaching in Ewam Choden to his brother, and was now preparing for his marriage to a young French experimental musician, Laetitia de Compiegne.

Through Thartse Khen's kindness, I had now received the final piece in the jigsaw of the Tsok-she ('assembly teaching') transmission of the *Path and its Fruit.* In short, I had received the requisite initiations from Phende Rinpoche. I had obtained the reading-transmission of Konchok Lhundrup's texts expounding *The Three Visions* and the *Three Tantras* from Karma Thinley Rinpoche. From H.H. Sakya Trizin I had received the oral explanation of the *Three Visions*, and now, finally, from Thartse Khen, I had obtained the oral explanation of the *Three Tantras.*

Equipped in this way, I went into a retreat on Hevajra and also meditated on the thirty-two contemplations of the *Inseparability of Samsara and Nirvana* presented in the *Three Tantras.* As some initial understanding began to arise in my mind, I felt that many obstacles were dissolving. As with *Mahamudra* and Great Perfection, meditating on this view both stabilised and clarified those experiences that had first arisen in my childhood, and gave me a great sense of confidence in the path. Consequently, over a number of years, I was able to complete the requisite retreat time and numbers of recitations for Konchok Lhundrup's six-limbed sadhana of Hevajra.

Sadly, in the November of that same autumn, H.H. Karmapa passed away in Chicago, where he had been receiving treatment for stomach cancer. Many years of trouble began for the Karma-Kagyu at that very time, although it was not immediately obvious that such a dire outcome was in prospect.

Shortly after His Holiness's death, his General Secretary, Damcho Yongdu, convened a meeting in which he announced the appointment of the four senior-most tulkus of the Karma-Kagyu tradition – Shamar Rinpoche, Situ Rinpoche, Gyaltsap Rinpoche and Jamgon Kongtrul Rinpoche – as regents supervising the tradition until the next Karmapa's recognition and enthronement. All were then in their late twenties, having been brought up by Karmapa himself in Rumtek monastery in Sikkim. The General Secretary's move was a little unusual, since it appears that nothing quite like this had been done before, leaving a question mark over its legitimacy. Thus, Shamar Rinpoche, himself the nephew of the 16th Karmapa, was able to dissolve this ad hoc arrangement within a couple of years.

I had met H.E. the 14th Shamar Rinpoche at a conference for European Kagyu Centres, held at the Kamalashila Institute near Bonn, earlier that year. On talking with him there, he had impressed me as a straightforward and dignified person. He had certainly handled the subsequent meeting, which featured a heated clash between Akong Tulku and Ole Nyidahl, with considerable skill. I requested him to visit us in Kagyu Ling. I had no idea how many years would pass before that request was fulfilled nor what would happen to the Karma-Kagyu tradition in the meantime.

Thanks to our newly established Sakya charitable trust, a couple of generous donations, including one from Steve Mulligan, and a bank-loan, we managed to purchase a house for Thinley Rinchen Ling in Bristol, in late 1981. It cost around £25,000. Thus it was particularly auspicious when, the following April, Phende Rinpoche made his fourth visit. During the course of this stay, he bestowed the initiation of the goddess Vajrayogini Naro Khechari on those who had already received the major initiation of Hevajra the previous year. This prerequisite reflected the Sakya insistence that one must have obtained initiation in the mandala of a mother-line anuttara deity before receiving the blessing-initiation of Vajrayogini, and although it is more usual for Chakrasamvara to serve in this role, Hevajra can be classed as both a nondual and a mother-line tantra.

Phende Rinpoche then gave me the reading-transmission for the extraordinary sadhana of the goddess and bestowed the esoteric instructions on the practice of her development and completion stages, known as *The Vajrayogini Teaching According to the Ultimate Secret Yoga*, composed in the sixteenth century by Jamyang Khyentse Wangchuk. This great master had held the Tsar transmission of the eleven yogas that had been received directly from the goddess herself by the siddha Narotapa, great Indian patriarch of both Sakya and Kagyu traditions. Since that time, this cycle of practice, through which one can 'travel' to Khechara, the realm of the dakinis, and there achieve supreme enlightenment, has been one of the chief elements of my daily practice. I would receive the initiation again from Phende Rinpoche and H.H. Sakya Trizin, as well as a further transmission on the eleven yogas from H.H. Sakya Trizin, and other transmissions belonging to this cycle from Karma Thinley Rinpoche.

While he was with us, Phende Rinpoche also managed to give the initiation of the siddha Virupa, the transmission for Jamyang Kunga Tenpai Gyaltsen's 'transference' connected with Amitabha and the initiation of Chenrezi-Mahamudra.

In October 1982, Kagyu Ling, along with the other Karma-Kagyu centres in Britain, was able to invite Gyaltsap Rinpoche, another of the 'four regents'. While in Manchester, he gave teachings on the *Thirty-Seven Practices* to the general public, and, to the members of Kagyu Ling, he gave Dusum Khyenpa's initiation of the mandala of the Five Taras. In private, he bestowed Karmapa Wangchuk Dorje's *Mahamudra Pointing a Finger at the Dharmakaya* upon me. Gyaltsap Rinpoche was a few years younger than the three other senior Kagyu Tulkus and seemed quite shy.

The first significant dharma event of the following year was Phende Rinpoche's visit to Bristol, which took place in March. On this occasion, he gave the two-day initiation of Chakrasamvara from the lineage of the siddha Luipa, in addition to teaching the *Nectar of Good Fortune*, a work composed by Jamgon Ngawang Legpa, one of his own masters, which detailed the *Path and its Fruit* view of 'the inseparability of samsara and nirvana'.

Meanwhile, at Easter of that same year, I made my third trip to Toronto, where Karma Thinley Rinpoche had just returned from Tibet. The chief teaching that I received during this trip was the transmission for Mipham Rinpoche's *Gateway to Knowledge*, an encyclopaedic work on Abhidharma and related topics that Rinpoche had originally wanted to teach in Kagyu Ling in 1977.

In this text and in his *Precious Lamp of Certainty*, Mipham Rinpoche presents a perspective that blends together the approaches of the Madhyamaka and Valid Cognition (Pramana) systems, as did Sakya Pandita nearly seven centuries earlier. As he himself declares, to understand both conventional and ultimate truths one needs the two types of reasoning supplied in the Valid Cognition and Madhyamaka systems respectively:

> The Valid Cognition reasoning that examines
>   conventional truth
> Is unmistaken about how one should engage [in virtue]
>   and avoid [sin].
> Specifically, this textual tradition of Valid Cognition
> Is the only way to acquire confidence
> In the Buddha and his teaching.
> On the other hand, the Madhyamaka of the Supreme
>   vehicle
> Elucidates a stainless type of Valid Cognition
> That is endowed with the ultimate reasoning that
>   determines the true nature of things.
> These two
> Are the wisdom eyes of a well-trained mind.

Thus, with Pramana, the functional truth of karma and rebirth can be validly established, and, with Madhyamaka, the delusion that these processes depend upon real unchanging selves or other truly existent entities is dispelled.

Once he had completed this transmission, Rinpoche decided that it would be auspicious for me to have a connection with his lineage of Vajrayogini Naro Khechari, and thus bestowed on me the reading-transmission for her extra-ordinary sadhana. He also took the opportunity to provide further teachings on Zhentong, by giving me the reading-transmission for the 8th Karmapa's *Correct Analysis of the Zhentong Madhyamaka*. During my stay, Rinpoche suggested that I give a short course on Tokme Zangpo's *Thirty-Seven Practices of a Bodhisattva* in Drubgyud Ling. The subsequent event was the first occasion that I had taught outside England. About twenty people, mostly Rinpoche's students from Toronto, attended the two nights of the course, which was held in the centre's compact shrine-room.

Following my return from Canada, I did a retreat on Vajrayogini and then carried on with various teachings in the centres. That year was busy with a number of new developments. In the spring, Martyn Samuels and Paul Rogers, who had been attending Thinley Rinchen Ling for some years, asked if they could establish a group in Exeter. Rinpoche gave it the name Sakya Thinley Namgyal Ling. Our group there has proved something of a stable feature in a local spiritual landscape notable for its neo-Buddhist enthusiasms.

1983 saw the launch of our publishing company, Ganesha Press. Named by Rinpoche after one of the most important Vajrayana wealth deities, Ganesha, or Ganapati, it was founded specifically to publish a translation of Chogye Trichen's *History of the Sakya Tradition*. Some years earlier, Phende Rinpoche and his wife had translated this from Tibetan into French and they both thought that an English version would be useful. Although our proof-reading for this book was not entirely adequate, it has been of some benefit to the Sakya tradition in the West.

That winter, Karma Thinley Rinpoche spent several months in Nepal. Chogye Trichen Rinpoche had requested that Rinpoche come to his monastery in Lumbini, the place of Lord Buddha's birth, to receive the initiations, transmissions and instructions of the entire fourteen volumes of *A Collection of Sadhanas.* This great collection of Vajrayana teachings had been compiled by Jamyang Khyentse Wangpo and Jamgon Loter Wangpo, towards the end of the nineteenth century, and was itself constructed around various pre-existing collections of initiations and instructions of the New Tantra traditions, such as the *Thirteen Golden Dharmas.* I had managed to raise some funds for Rinpoche to put towards his offerings for these teachings, as he was one of the two main sponsors, along with Zimok Rinpoche.

At about this time, our dharma activities were renewed in Liverpool, when Geoffrey Ashmore, who had recently returned from Lumbini, together with others, followed up the work begun by Mike Wake a few years earlier. From Rinpoche's original list of centre names, I chose Shedrup Ling for the group that sprang up there. Despite passing problems, it has maintained a presence in the city down to the present day.

Thrangu Rinpoche returned for his third visit in early 1984. He bestowed the initiation of Milarepa, and then, over the three subsequent days, he gave the reading-transmission of the famous *Rain of Wisdom: Songs of the Kagyu Gurus.* Thrangu Rinpoche's visit was quickly followed by that of Phende Rinpoche to Bristol. There, Phende Rinpoche gave the Vajrayogini initiation again and that of Gonkar (often known, somewhat paradoxi-

cally, as 'White Mahakala'). This wealth-deity and protector had been transmitted originally in the Shangpa
Kagyu school established by the 11th century Tibetan
master, Khyungpo Naljor. Phende Rinpoche also managed to fit in a short visit to our group in Exeter, where
he gave the initiation and teaching of Vajrasattva Heruka.

A few days later, I flew to Germany, at the invitation of
a number of dharma-groups. My first stop was Munich,
where I gave some teachings from Dampa Sangye that
I had received from Rinpoche in Toronto some time
earlier. Although Vajrayana Buddhism was growing in
Germany, after many years during which Theravada
and Zen had attracted most involvement, there did not
seem to be much interest in what I was teaching. From
Munich, I travelled on to Augsburg and Erlangen, in
both of which cities I gave public talks. The final part
of my trip was to Karma Lodro Ling, a small centre
located between Tubingen and Stuttgart. There, I gave
teachings on a short text by Patrul Rinpoche that I had
received from Ato Rinpoche some years earlier.

The centre was close to the Black Forest area, and we
drove out to see Calw, the place where Herman Hesse
spent his childhood. He was a man who had looked a little
further than most other modern writers into the places
of darkness and light. I hope his books are not forgotten;
young people could learn quite a bit from them.

At Easter, thanks to a sabbatical term from my academic post, I was able to enter into three months of
retreat practice on Vajrayogini Naro Khechari. I had to
remain at home to do it but it was free from problems. I
was able to finish this serious retreat shortly before our
son, Michael, was born in mid-July. I gave him the name
Kunga Sengge from the list that Rinpoche had given to
me earlier.

Two months later, H.H. Sakya Trizin returned to England; it had been six years since his previous visit. On this occasion, His Holiness gave five days of teachings in Bristol, commencing with a short course on *Parting from the Four Attachments*. This general teaching was followed by the initiations of Dzambhala and Manjushri Arapatsana from Bari Lotsava, the initiation of Chenrezi-Mahamudra and the initiation of Amitayus from the lineage of Tangtong Gyalpo. At the end of his stay, His Holiness advised me to study Gorampa Sonam Sengge's *Discriminating the Madhyamaka View* in order to deepen my understanding of how Sakya philosophical theory is to be distinguished from both the Gelug Prasangika and Zhentong versions of Madhyamaka.

Subsequently, I developed a great confidence in Gorampa's presentation, which I have never lost, not solely due to his impeccable fidelity to reasoning and scripture, but also because he showed that the philosophical and contemplative approaches dovetail perfectly. He placed a particular emphasis on how the non-conceptual, unelaborated nature of the Madhyamaka view transcends an intellectual apprehension of emptiness as a mere negation. Although this latter understanding of emptiness is maintained by some philosophers, it can trap one in an endless proliferation of concepts 'about emptiness', whereas, through alternating analytical and non-conceptual meditation, one prepares for the unmediated experience of reality as it is, which experience will be brought about rapidly, if one applies the skilful practices of Vajrayana.

At Easter 1985, Phende Rinpoche came for the seventh time. On this occasion, the main focus of his teaching was the *Fifty Verses on the Lama* composed by Bhavideva, for which he used the commentary of Tsarchen Losal Gyamtso, entitled *Opening the Door to Precious Accomplish-ments*. In addition to this major work on the relation-ship with our tantric masters, Rinpoche bestowed the initiation of Vajrapani Bhutadamara and some teaching on the Madhyamaka view, drawing upon the very text of Gorampa that His Holiness had praised. A few weeks later, I went to visit him in France, where he gave me the transmissions and instructions for the extensive rituals of the dharma protectors of the Sakya and Ngor tradi-tions and the reading-transmission for Gorampa's com-mentary on *Parting from the Four Attachments*.

Meanwhile, alongside this dharma activity, there had been some developments in my academic career. First, in 1980, in addition to my post at the Polytechnic, I had been appointed an honorary lecturer in Tibetan Religions at the University of Manchester. Then, in 1984, *The Penguin Dictionary of Religions*, a major work of reference, was published, containing, inter alia, various articles that I had written on Tibetan religion. Finally, in September 1985, I submitted my Ph.D. thesis and received my doctorate several months later, much to Rinpoche's pleasure at least. Some years earlier, Trungpa Rinpoche had boasted to him that fifty of his students possessed Ph.Ds. Now, finally, Rinpoche had one such student! My father was also modestly pleased, as he now had two sons who could be called doctors, my brother having qualified in medicine.

It turned out to be the high water of my academic career, such as it was. For one thing, I could never shake off a certain personal ambivalence about the academic study of dharma. For another, I was too connected to my home-town of Manchester to chase jobs anywhere else, even if my heart had been in it. So, for the next fifteen years, it made more sense to carry on as I was, working across the re-baptised Manchester Metropolitan

University (formerly Manchester Polytechnic) and my own alma mater, The University of Manchester. I wasn't going anywhere fast.

In December 1985, the meditation master Bokar Rinpoche came to Manchester for a few days on his way to Samye Ling. While with us, he gave the initiation of the dharma-protectors Dorje Bernagchen and Rangjung Gyalmo, and a detailed overview of the Shangpa Kagyu tradition. As Kalu Rinpoche's regent, he was especially learned in that system of practice, since his master had done more than anyone in the twentieth century to preserve the key Shangpa transmissions. It was also during these days that Bokar Rinpoche gave me the reading-transmission for Jamgon Kongtrul's *The Complete Liberation of the Three Realms: A Guide to the Completion Stage of Konchok Chindu,* the practice of which was very rare, in contrast with the deity-yoga practices of this system. In any event, this completed my receipt of the teachings belonging to the Konchog Chindu cycle.

1986 brought major changes to Kagyu Ling, when Karma Thinley Rinpoche announced that he wished to sell the building to raise funds for a new project. It appears that during the transmission of *A Collection of Sadhanas*, Rinpoche had finally decided to establish a monastic institution in Bodhanath, close to the Great Stupa. Subsequently, one of Rinpoche's Tibetan disciples, Tsering Chodron, had given him the funds to buy a piece of land there. However, to be able to build anything, Rinpoche needed the extra financial resources that only the sale of his property in Manchester would release.

Rinpoche's decision to employ these funds in this project should not really have been surprising, since he had always been dedicated to the maintenance of the monastic life. Over the next thirty-plus years of its existence (to date), under Rinpoche's careful tutelage, this institution would become a place where young nuns – first from East Tibet and, later on, from the Dolpo region of Nepal – could train as ritual practitioners and meditators.

An unintended consequence was that Kagyu Ling was now homeless and would remain so for fourteen years. Thanks to dedicated people like Angela and Phil Brady and Marion and Glyn Davies, we could carry on a limited programme. However, we lost impetus, and, when we could finally acquire a property in 2000, Kagyu Ling would effectively be beginning again, twenty-five years after its initial founding. Nonetheless, we could take some pride both in what Rinpoche was able to achieve with these resources and in the continuing flow of support that we would provide for the nunnery. Thus, over the long term, it turned out for the best, including for Kagyu Ling itself.

At Easter time of that year, Phende Rinpoche visited. Staying firstly in Bristol, he again gave the initiation of Vajrapani Bhutadamara, but, on this occasion, also gave the guiding instructions for the practice, which had been composed by Zhuchen Tsultrim Rinchen, a great seventeenth-century Sakya scholar from Dege in Eastern Tibet. At my invitation, he then travelled to Manchester, where he gave the initiation of The Lords of the Three Families (Manjushri, Chenrezi and Vajrapani), and bestowed upon me the reading-transmission for Maitreya's *Discriminating the Middle and Extremes,* together with its commentary by Khenpo Zhenga.

In August, I made a fairly lengthy visit to Karma Thinley Rinpoche in Toronto. There, I received reading-transmission for Sonam Tsemo's *General Presentation of the Tantra Sets*, a major work on the methods and structure of the Vajrayana and the history of the tantras, generally seen as part of the entire *Path and its Fruit* textual collection. This was followed by the series of Kadam spiritual instructions, including the famous 'One Hundred Mind-Trainings', from Jamgon Kongtrul's *Treasury of Spiritual Instructions,* plus two further Zhentong works. The first of these was *A Guide to the Zhentong View* by Jamgon Kongtrul himself, and the second was Karmapa Rangjung Dorje's famed *Discriminating between Consciousness and Primordial Wisdom*. Rinpoche had recently composed a new commentary upon the latter work, entitled the *Lamp that Dispels Darkness*, and this he bestowed upon me with the injunction that I translate it from Tibetan.

As on my previous visit to Toronto, I gave a short dharma-course in Drubgyud Ling, which was, as before, mainly attended by Rinpoche's own disciples, but also included the translator Chris Fynn, who had studied for some time with the late Kunu Rinpoche, 'the last of the Maha Panditas'. Rinpoche's small group in Ottawa also invited me to give teaching on the *Seven Points of Mind-Training*. The group there was run by Rinpoche's first Canadian student, Elizabeth Diwedi, who had actually met him in India in 1965.

It would be twenty years before I would return to North America. Now, my travels would begin to take me to Asia, where H.H. Sakya Trizin was already based, and where Rinpoche himself would begin to establish his activities. It must have been the right time for me to turn to the East.

Chapter Four
Reading the Signs

This new phase began in late December of that same year, when, accompanied by two students from Bristol, Mick Lund and Rosie Warwick, I travelled to India to spend some time with H.H. Sakya Trizin. After a couple of days in Delhi, attempting to adjust to India, we travelled northwards. At this time, His Holiness had two main residences, the principal one being located in the Rajpur district of Dehra Dun, one hundred and sixty miles from Delhi, and a second, situated close to the Sakya refugee settlement at Puruwala and about fifty miles from Dehra Dun.

His Holiness's palace there is adjacent to Sakya Thubten Namgyal Ling monastery and the Sakya refugee settlement. The surrounding land is given over to agriculture and forest, with the foothills of the Western Himalayas just beginning to rise out of the plain. There, in his private shrine-room, His Holiness bestowed the esoteric initiations and teachings of the *Thirteen Golden Dharmas*, unique to the Sakya tradition. Some of these deities, such as the three dakinis of Naro, Maitri and Indrabhuti, enable the practitioner to obtain the ultimate spiritual accomplishment, while others, such as the three 'Great Reds', lead to mundane accomplishments such as prosperity and protection.

As I had already received Naro Dakini twice, on this occasion His Holiness only gave the other two of the major dakinis of the cycle, Indra Dakini and Maitri Dakini. Then he bestowed Ganapati and Kamaraja, two of the three 'Great Reds' of the cycle, substituting Chenrezi Simhanada for the third, Kurukulla. He would give me the latter's initiation a couple of decades later. Next he bestowed the three 'Minor Reds', Tara-Kurukulla, Tinu-Devi and Vasudhara, all of whom also grant the magnetising accomplishment. Finally, he bestowed the three deities who remove various obstacles, Simhamukha, Black Manjushri and Garuda, as well as Pranasadhana Dzambhala. The only other people attending these initiations were His Holiness's two sons, H.E. Ratna Vajra and H.E. Gyana Vajra, as well as Chiwang Tulku, an old friend of Karma Thinley Rinpoche and a practitioner famous for his mastery of Vajrayogini.

Ratna Rinpoche was twelve years old and was studying at this time with his tutor, Gen Rinchen Zangpo, a long-term member of the Phodrang household. He had recently finished his first retreat, the month-long practice of Vajrapani Bhutadamara. Away from the initiations and his studies, Rinpoche delighted in playing cricket, and impromptu matches became a frequent occurrence during our stay there. Since so few people came to the palace during this period, I was also able to receive various reading-transmissions from His Holiness. These included the extensive and condensed fire pujas for Vajrayogini, the Vajrayogini mandala puja and two 'transference' practices related to her. On returning to England, I would accomplish the fire puja of Vajrayogini and a one-week retreat on Tara-Kurukulla.

At Thinley Rinchen Ling, I began teaching a year-long course on Shantideva's *Entering the Path of a Bodhisattva*. Then, at Easter time, Phende Rinpoche came in fulfilment of the promise he made the previous year to give the esoteric teachings of White Tara. Firstly, he bestowed the initiation from Bari Lotsava and then he gave the guiding instructions for the practice composed by Ngawang Legdrup from the lineage of Tsarchen Losal Gyamtso. Over the years, I managed to complete the full number of recitations for the goddess in retreat.

This was the last occasion on which Phende Rinpoche visited Bristol. However, my gratitude for his kindness can hardly be expressed. Even now, many years later, his teachings are still present in my daily practice, along with those of His Holiness and Karma Thinley Rinpoche.

That summer of 1987, my daughter Miriam was born and received the name Kunga Chonyi from His Holiness. At Christmas of the same year, I made another trip to Germany, visiting groups in Braunschweig and Hamburg. In the latter city, the Kagyu centre was, at that time, one of the largest in Germany. I gave teachings there on the *Eight Verses of Mind-Training* to the followers of Lama Ole Nyidahl. It was not a teaching found in their regular syllabus.

In March 1988, Rinpoche and I travelled to Nepal. We were accompanied by Mick Lund, who had volunteered to help supervise the construction of Rinpoche's monastery. The piece of land that Rinpoche had been able to buy was located about two-thirds of a mile from the Great Stupa of Bodhanath in Kathmandu, the nation's capital. Bodhanath itself was an area rapidly filling with new monasteries, side-by-side with the carpet factories and grand houses owned by wealthy Tibetan entrepreneurs.

During the three weeks that I stayed with Rinpoche in Bodhanath, much of the time was taken up in planning for the monastery, to be named Tegchen Legshay Ling, a name reflecting the monastery established by the first Karma Thinleypa in South Tibet, back in the early sixteenth century. It was fortunate for the project that Mick (Kunga Gyaltsen) could stay on to help with some of the work. His years of experience in the English building trade rendered him ideally qualified to supervise the Bihari work-force employed in the construction of the nunnery.

Each evening, Rinpoche gave me some of Patrul Rinpoche's *Words of My Perfect Master*, until he had completed the entire transmission. I was especially happy to receive this, because Rinpoche and other lamas had regularly praised this famous work to me over the years. Although it serves as a commentary on the preliminary practices of the *Longchen Nyingtik*, its five hundred and sixty pages are a repository of wonderfully detailed and evocative teachings, making you feel as if you are receiving it directly from Patrul Rinpoche himself, in nineteenth-century Kham.

Together with Rinpoche, I was also able to pay a short visit to Chogye Tri Rinpoche in his Maitreya temple. This small monastery belonging to the Tsarpa tradition, of which Tri Rinpoche was the head, was located just facing the Great Stupa itself, and contained a grand statue of the eponymous bodhisattva. It was an especially inspiring occasion to see my teacher with one of his own masters, about whom he had told me so many stories over the years.

It reminded me that Patrul Rinpoche compares the master to a sandalwood tree and his students to the non-scented trees surrounding it. Little by little, over the years, the students become influenced by the lama's blessings and his qualities 'transfer' to the disciples, just as the surrounding trees eventually become imbued with sandalwood scent, due to their proximity to the sandalwood tree. In the relationship between Chogye Tri and Rinpoche I could see a living demonstration of this process.

In July, Rinpoche flew to England to give two weeks of teachings before returning to Toronto. His programme began in Manchester, where he gave the initiations of Milarepa and Vajravarahi, and then moved to Bristol where he gave the initiations of Padmasambhava and Maitreya.

While this period of teaching was happening, Karma Lodro Ling in Germany invited Rinpoche to visit and bestow initiations. Rinpoche was happy to agree to their request, hoping that there might be some interest in supporting Legshay Ling. We spent four days in Stuttgart, where we were met by beautiful weather. While we were there, Rinpoche gave the initiation of Konchok Chindu and the group of four Kadam deities (Shakyamuni, Chenrezi, Tara and Achala) to the thirty or so people who attended. However, no particular pledges of support for Rinpoche's nunnery were gathered.

On our return to England, Rinpoche gave me the *Explanation of Vajravarahi*, a set of teachings on the outer, inner and secret practices of the goddess, composed by the famous Kagyu historian Pawo Tsuklak Trengwa. He also gave me the reading-transmission for Karmapa Rangjung Dorje's famous Zhentong work, *Showing the Essence of the Tathagata*, together with its commentary composed by Jamgon Kongtrul.

Rinpoche named two new groups in the course of his visit to Britain that summer. On the first occasion, Rana and Tony Lister brought a request that Rinpoche bless our new group in Birmingham. Rinpoche agreed to this and gave it the name Sakya Goshak Choling, in memory of the two great fifteenth-century Sakya philosophers – Gorampa Sonam Sengge and Shakya Chogden. Then, a day or two later, Patrick Wilkinson and John Rowan came from the former mill-town of Colne in Northern Lancashire with a similar request. To this group, Rinpoche gave the name Kagyu Dzong.

Rinpoche's final act, before returning to Canada, was to give me the authority to bestow Vajrayana initiations and consecrations. He conferred this in response to a request made by Rana Lister, who wished to receive the initiation of Machik Labdron. In doing so, Rinpoche cited the retreats that I had accomplished for the Vajrayogini and Konchog Chindu cycles as sufficient qualification. So, in this way, he placed upon me the responsibility to work for others through teaching the profound view and bestowing the blessings of Vajrayana, which empower practitioners to meditate on the deities set forth in the tantras as the swift way to accomplishment of our spiritual aims.

It might be that this conferral of authority was a small sign of the continuing transmission of dharma as it moves from East to West. It also reflected, perhaps, Rinpoche's conviction that his own most important sphere of activity would be in the East. Indeed, although he had successfully established Kampo Gangra Drubgyud Ling and Marpa Gompa in Canada, Rinpoche's efforts in the U.S.A. had come to nought. Even his two summers of teaching at the Naropa Institute in Boulder had been somewhat disappointing, with the participants finding Rinpoche's teaching on *The Jewel Ornament* less appealing than the usual instructions provided there.

Although Rinpoche had entrusted these increased duties to me, I felt that I should bide my time for six months before carrying out such activities. It seemed to me that delaying a little would create auspicious circumstances, whereas acting too precipitately might generate difficulties. I thought about the great seriousness with which Patrul Rinpoche considers the necessary qualifications of the lama. I also remembered the words of Tsarchen Losal Gyamtso:

> The modern custom of bestowing the teachings
> without thought, immediately they are requested, is
> like throwing meat in front of dogs.[1]

Consequently, I taught Gampopa's *Jewel Ornament of Liberation* for Kagyu Ling, and, while that course stretched through the winter and into the following spring, I gave Geshe Chekhawa's *Seven Points of Mind-Training* in Bristol. Then, finally, in March 1989, after completing a seven-day retreat on the practice, I actually bestowed the initiation of Machik Labdron, as had been requested. Since Kagyu Ling was homeless at that time, the initiation took place in the Manchester Bridge Club, a venue more usually occupied by people like the late actor Omar Sharif and other roving gamblers.

At the end of that same month, we hosted H.H. Sakya Trizin on his third visit to Bristol. Regrettably, on this occasion, His Holiness's time with us was rather limited, itself an indication of the many new demands being made upon him. However, he was able to bestow two initiations. The first of these was the torma initiation of Vajrakilaya from the Khon lineage. On the following day, His Holiness bestowed Vajrapani Bhutadamara, and in the evening he gave a well-attended public teaching.

Around the same time, Ganesha Press published *Diamond Sky*, a brief introduction for those new to the dharma. It had been written the previous summer on the island of Corfu, a place where you can gaze out over the wine-dark sea and wonder when Dionysos will turn up with his dolphins and his maenads to dance on the circus sand. My book itself was based on the works of Sakya Pandita and Ngorchen Konchog Lhundrup, and made no concessions to modern tastes in style or content. Rinpoche kindly supplied a foreword for this work.

Immediately after this publication, I travelled to Karma Lodro Ling, where I began to teach Karmapa Mikyo Dorje's *Correct Analysis of the Zhentong Madhyamaka System*. It would take three more visits to complete this course. Then, returning to England in mid-April, I made a retreat on Chenrezi, before giving the initiation for this practice in Bristol. It was just at this time that Kalu Rinpoche passed away in his monastery in Sonada.

Some years earlier, Karma Thinley Rinpoche had urged me to establish a centre in France or Germany. As it happened, that August we were finally able to fulfil this injunction, when the Thinley Rinchen Ling Trust, aided by a generous donation from Rana and Tony Lister, acquired some land in the Dordogne region of South-West France for the sum of £20,000. The property, initially comprising two barns and two acres of land, was situated in an area of hills and forests, close to the market town of Le Bugue. It would require years of work, further donations and the acquisition of more land to make a functioning centre there. Nevertheless, Rinpoche was pleased, and named it Sakya Changlochen Ling after Alakavati (in Tibetan, *Changlochen*), the land of Vajrapani, the bodhisattva responsible for transmission of the tantras. This name had actually been suggested to Rinpoche by Chogye Tri Rinpoche, who had told him to use it for a centre.

It seems that it was a time of naming, because it was also then that Rinpoche decided on 'Dechen' as the general name for the small collection of centres and groups that I had founded under his authority. The name itself originated in a poem that he had composed in a dream. On awakening, Rinpoche could only remember the first line: 'Great bliss (in Tibetan, *De-chen*) is the antidote to laziness', but he took this as a good sign and so suggested that we should adopt it.

In fact, this name is no more than a convenient designation for our network; it does not signify that our centres and groups are part of any 'movement' or constitute an independent dharma tradition. Simply put, some of our Dechen centres and groups belong to the Sakya tradition and thus look to Dolma Phodrang for their ultimate authority, while some belong to Kagyu tradition and look to the line of the Karmapas. In other words, the two-fold nature of our community simply reflects Rinpoche's original wish to serve the two traditions.

Over in the academic world, that autumn, *Religion*, the academic journal of religious studies, published my paper *Offering the Body: the practice of gCod in Tibetan Buddhism*. I had previously delivered a draft of this paper at a conference on *The Body* hosted by the Department of Religion at the University of Lancaster. Another byproduct of my academic work came about, at this time, when two ex-Gelug followers, Gary Beesley and Neville Richardson, started to attend my University lectures as undocumented students. They would bring their own unique qualities to our small dharma community, with Gary producing some fine books on Buddhism for schools, and Neville playing an important role in our support for Angulimala, the Buddhist prison chaplaincy founded by the English monk Ven Khemadhammo.

On his return from Legshay Ling earlier in the summer, Rinpoche had asked me to travel to Kathmandu, to check on the ongoing construction work at Tegchen Legshay Ling. I was happy to fulfil his request and so, on the 21st of December, I flew to Nepal. The flight was immediately after the funeral of my father; he had died at the age of seventy-five. My father had seen much in his life – some things difficult even to imagine – broken bodies stretching from the beaches at Dunkirk to the battle of Monte Cassino. I thought of this when I made prayers at the Great Stupa and every day from then on.

Legshay Ling itself was still partially under development when I arrived, but Rinpoche's maternal uncle, Pön Namkha Dorje, was in residence there with his family and attendants. Formerly the chief minister of the king of Nangchen, and disciple of the 16th Karmapa, Namkha Dorje had established a refugee settlement in Mainpat in the central Indian state of Orissa for his Bongsar clan and followers. Now he had moved to Legshay Ling, together with his wife Demtso and daughter Sremo Tsodi Bongsar, to lend his authority to his nephew's project.

During my visit, I commissioned a life-size statue of Vajrayogini for the nunnery; later I would have it painted with gold leaf. As a further act of homage to Vajrayogini, I made a trip to Pharping on the southern rim of the Kathmandu valley, where I made offerings at her temple. It was in this very place that Narotapa's disciples, the Phamtingpa brothers, had maintained her rituals nine-hundred years earlier. Their descendants still control the temple today. I also made prayers in the Asura cave, where Guru Rinpoche had meditated on Vajrakilaya.

Shortly before I had left England, Rinpoche had suggested to me that I invite Chogye Trichen Rinpoche to Legshay Ling. A few days before my departure from Nepal, he came for lunch, together with his distinguished American translator, Dr Cyrus Stearns. During the meal, Tri Rinpoche talked to me about the continuing search for the incarnation of the 16th Karmapa. He told me that he had been very happy to report to Shamar Rinpoche on an auspicious dream concerning H.H. Karmapa's rebirth that he had experienced. Apparently, it had proved quite helpful. Some years down the line, Chogye Tri's words would acquire a special significance for me.

In contrast to the two previous years, 1990 was fairly quiet. In the spring, I accomplished a retreat on Manjushri, the embodiment of the transcendental wisdom of all Buddhas, before flying to Germany. There, I continued with my teaching in Karma Lodro Ling. A little while later, I gave the initiation of Sakya Pandita in Bristol and then entered into a short retreat on Konchok Chindu. It was the first time I had accomplished a retreat on this cycle since the winter of 1977.

In August, a number of people camped on our newly acquired land in the Dordogne. By good fortune, it turned out that Jamgon Kongtrul Rinpoche was visiting the nearby Dhagpo Kagyu Ling at the very same time. I took the opportunity to make a short journey by car to see him. Over tea, Kongtrul Rinpoche acceded to my request to visit us in Britain and also gave his blessing to the publication of *Garland of Gold*, my forthcoming work on early Kagyu history, for which Karma Thinley Rinpoche had written the foreword. I did not realise at the time that it would be the last occasion that I would meet Jamgon Rinpoche.

1991 began with some days of teaching on the *Fifty Verses of the Lama*, together with the initiation of Manjushri Arapatsana in Bristol. Subsequently, for the remainder of the year, my programme there was focussed on Sakya Pandita's *Elucidating the Thought of the Sage*, while in Manchester I gave teachings on Jamgon Kongtrul's *Great Path of Awakening* and the initiation of Konchok Chindu. Subsequently, I would teach *The Bliss Path of Liberation*, the Konchok Chindu preliminaries, to some students.

After a visit to Germany in April, I completed a seven-day retreat on Amitabha, my first on this deity since 1977. Then, a month later, Rinpoche and I travelled to Nepal. While I was there, at Rinpoche's suggestion, I taught *Parting from the Four Attachments* to a group of Nepalis. They had recently converted to Buddhism under the guidance of Rinpoche and Chogye Trichen Rinpoche.

The month of August saw my second visit to Changlochen. Although still primitive, the conditions were sufficient for me to give the initiations of the important wealth-deity Yellow Dzambala, from Bari Lotsava, and Green Tara for protection from all fears. We also redrew the administrative structure of Sakya Thinley Rinchen Ling, with Carl Rogers and David Armstrong stepping into the administration.

The following month, I received the news that Dilgo Khyentse Rinpoche had passed away in Bhutan. As had happened with H.H. Karmapa and Kalu Rinpoche, another of the figures from my early years in dharma had now gone. However, one of my two main living masters, H.H. Sakya Trizin, came that October to give a public teaching in Bristol, followed by the longevity-initiation of Amitayus from the lineage of Tangtong Gyalpo. Then, at my request, he gave the initiation of Vajrayogini to suitably qualified students. Although it was a rather short visit, His Holiness also found time to visit our group in Exeter. There, he gave a well-attended public talk.

It was around this time that I began to travel to Eastern Europe. Until the fall of Communism in 1989, there had been little opportunity for dharma to grow there, although Vajrayana had been present in Russian territories, at least, ever since the seventeenth century, due to their Kalmyk and Buryat populations. However, things began to change now, with dharma teachers visiting such countries as Poland, Romania and Hungary, thanks to the easing of the totalitarian restrictions on religion.

In December 1991, I visited Bulgaria at the joint invitation of The Bulgarian-Tibetan Friendship Group and a rather odd organisation which called itself 'The Ashoka Foundation', but, as subsequently became clear, was a front for The Unification Church. It was a bitterly cold time but hundreds of people attended my public talks in the cities of Sofia and Plovdiv. However, the numbers were a little misleading; the big crowds would fade away quickly after the novelty of attending such lectures wore off.

Nevertheless, I agreed to return the following summer to fulfil the requests of a group of people for more extensive teaching. We would see how this would all turn out. In the meantime, in the political world of dharma, storm clouds were gathering.

Out of the blue, in March, in common with many centres around the world, Kagyu Ling received a letter from a Tibetan group styling itself 'The Dege Association'. Their letter contained thinly veiled complaints about Shamar Rinpoche and the delay in the recognition of the 17th Karmapa. It also called upon Situ Rinpoche to recognise the new Karmapa unilaterally, something which was somewhat surprising, as he ranked below Shamar Rinpoche in the hierarchy. This letter was merely a harbinger of problems to come, and followed a steady circulation of negative briefing in Karma-Kagyu circles against Shamar Rinpoche, blaming him for the fact that the four tulkus had not been able to produce any encouraging news concerning the rebirth of H.H. Karmapa.

That same month, I accomplished a seven-day retreat on Sangye Menla and then went on to visit Karma Lodro Ling to begin teaching the 3rd Karmapa's *Discriminating between Consciousness and Primordial Wisdom,* supported by Rinpoche's own commentary, the *Lamp that Dispels Darkness*. Returning from Germany, I travelled to a course that had been arranged in West Wales. About fifty people attended and, at the end of the week, I gave the initiation of Sangye Menla.

A couple of weeks later came the news of Jamgon Kongtrul Rinpoche's untimely death in a car crash in India. From that point, things moved fast in the Karma-Kagyu world. Within a few weeks, reports reached us that Situ Rinpoche and Gyaltsap Rinpoche had recognised a boy from Eastern Tibet as the 17th Karmapa, naming him Orgyen Thinley Dorje. Yet although Situ Rinpoche's candidate enjoyed widespread support among Tibetans, Shamar Rinpoche had withheld his agreement, citing Situ Rinpoche's inability or unwillingness to produce the prediction letter, allegedly left with him by the 16th Karmapa, for investigation. By the time I gave the transmission of 'transference' in Manchester in early July, we had been sent photographs of Orgyen Thinley Dorje, and the scene was set for years of struggle between the rival camps of Situ Rinpoche and Shamar Rinpoche. A few days after the 'transference' transmission, I made my second visit to Bulgaria. Arrangements had been made for me to give a course on *Parting from the Four Attachments*. It was held in a small semi-abandoned Orthodox Christian nunnery, close to Turnovo, the old capital of the country in the centuries before the Islamic occupation. During these teachings, I gave Refuge to several people and concluded the course with the initiation of Chenrezi-Mahamudra. Despite some difficulties during those days, the evident seriousness of a few people convinced me to continue for the time being with these visits to the ancient land of Orpheus.

Shortly after my return to England, Karma Thinley Rinpoche arrived to give a series of initiations from the first three volumes of *A Collection of Sadhanas*. Rinpoche began by giving the three 'white' long life deities: White Tara, White Amitayus and White Saraswati. He followed these by bestowing the initiations of Machik Drupai Gyalmo's Amitayus according to the Tsarpa tradition, Machik Drupai Gyalmo's Amitayus according to the Sakya tradition, Amitayus according to the Drikung Kagyu tradition, the Nirmanakaya Amitayus according to the Sakya tradition, Amitayus according to the Taklung Kagyu tradition, Amitayus according to the Rechung lineage, Tangtong Gyalpo's Amitayus and Hayagriva conjoined, and Tangtong Gyalpo's Amitayus from the conjoined 'oral', 'treasure' and 'pure vision' lineages.

In addition to these various longevity initiations, Rinpoche also found the time to bestow three further initiations from this collection – the initiations of Chenrezi-Mahamudra, Manjushri Arapatsana from the Bari Lotsava tradition and Manjushri Sakya Pandita. To conclude this cycle of teachings, Rinpoche and I led the gana-puja of Konchok Chindu. Privately, at this time, Rinpoche expressed his wish to avoid being drawn into the contest between Shamar Rinpoche and Situ Rinpoche over the recognition of Karmapa. A fierce conflict had now erupted at Rumtek in Sikkim, the headquarters of the Karma-Kagyu tradition in exile. It was not looking like an easy future.

In the autumn, *Religion* published my paper *Buddhadharma and Contemporary Ethics*, which outlined, for an academic audience, the discomfort that the traditional Buddhist characterisation of abortion as non-virtuous might cause some Western enthusiasts for the religion, if they were ever to hear it. This continued the themes that I had discussed in my booklet, *A Circle for the Protection of the Unborn*, published some years earlier by Ganesha Press.

Shortly after the publication of this paper, I returned to Karma Lodro Ling in Germany. While I was there, I was given a copy of the *Karmapa Files*, a collection of documents concerning the recognition of Karmapa that had just been published by disciples of Shamar Rinpoche. It made interesting reading, not least because it was consistent with what I had heard some years previously from Chogye Tri Rinpoche.

Early in the new year of 1993, I travelled again to Bulgaria, where a translation of my work, *Diamond Sky*, had been brought out by a local publisher. To mark its publication, I gave talks in Sofia and Varna. There were heavy snowfalls, making travel to Eastern Bulgaria for the second of these launches exceptionally difficult. Varna itself was the rather pretty Black Sea port from where Count Dracula had sailed to Yorkshire – according to Bram Stoker, at least. Just up the coast and over the border was the Romanian city of Constanta, where Ovid had definitely passed his days in exile. Back in Sofia, I gave the initiation of Green Tara from the lineage of Atisha to our recently formed group there. It had about half a dozen members.

This trip to Bulgaria was followed by a visit to Nepal with Karma Thinley Rinpoche at Easter, which enabled me to take our annual contribution to Legshay Ling in person. After we had been there for a few days, Rinpoche gave me the first nine initiations of Bari Lotsava's *One Hundred Sadhanas* (Bari Gyatsa), one of the most prized collections of teachings of the Sakya tradition. It had been collected in the early twelfth century, by the Tibetan master Rinchen Drakpa, the Translator from Bari, who had spent some time in India studying with such masters as Vajrasanapada. Subsequently, he had passed it to his disciple, Sachen Kunga Nyingpo, first of the Five Venerable Masters of Sakya.

At the end of the nineteenth century, Bari Lotsava's collection had been included as part of *A Collection of Sadhanas*. Subsequently, *The One Hundred Sadhanas*, together with the rest of this fourteen-volume collection, had been transmitted by their redactor, Jamgon Loter Wangpo, to the 39th Sakya Trizin, Dakshul Thinley Rinchen. He, in turn, transmitted them to his sister, Pema Thinley Dudul Wangmo. She had later given them to Zimok Rinpoche of Nalendra monastery, who, in turn, passed them to the late Chogye Trichen Rinpoche. In 1983, Chogye Trichen Rinpoche transmitted it to Karma Thinley Rinpoche. Now, over the next five years, I would receive the entire seventy-six initiations of Bari Lotsava from Rinpoche.

In England, that year of 1993, I taught Nagarjuna's *Friendly Letter*, and gave the initiations of Bari Lotsava's Yellow Dzambhala and Chogyur Dechen Lingpa's Secret Drop Vajrakilaya. When we travelled to Changlochen, in August, I taught the first part of Sonam Tsemo's *General Presentation of the Tantra Sets* to about fifty people who had made the journey from England.

Early in the next year, a powerful sign occurred, though it was one that I did not fully understand at the time. In the course of a dream, I saw the goddess Kakhashya,

who guards the eastern direction in the protective cor-
don of Vajrayogini. As I looked towards her, she moved
from the periphery to the centre of the mandala. There
she took up her place.

Chapter Five
Mirror of Answers

Everywhere one travels, one finds suffering. Sometimes it can seem like it's endless. It's there amongst the rich and poor, the strong and the weak. Every place has been touched by it. No government can eliminate it, and no doctor has the cure for it. You might try to hide yourself from it, or you might rage against it, but, either way, it's useless. You might as well be offended by water for being wet.

At the same time, one must acknowledge that, due to the ripening of the seeds established by virtuous actions, moments of joy also come to pass in this world. Such happy experiences should inspire us to redouble our efforts on the bodhisattva's altruistic path, for, as Shantideva says:

> Whatever happiness there is in this world
> All comes from wanting others to be happy.[2]

I was reminded of these considerations many times over the next few years. They were to be years full of travel, beginning that Easter, 1994, when I embarked on a month-long trip. It started in Poland, where I had been invited by the Karma-Kagyu group in Torun, a University town some hundred-and-fifty miles north-west of Warsaw and the birth-place of Copernicus. I was happy to be in Poland; it was the native soil of Joseph Conrad and Isaac Bashevis Singer – both masters of the tell-tale heart.

As I discovered, the Polish followers of the Karma-Kagyu were divided into two factions: the Diamond Way of Lama Ole Nydahl and the Kamtsang group established by Tenga Rinpoche, the former vajra-master of Rumtek monastery, who supported Situ Rinpoche's Karmapa candidate. Members of both groups attended the initiations of Machik Labdron and Manjushri that I gave in Torun.

Coincidentally, it was there that I received the news from the Diamond Way that Shamar Rinpoche had discovered a candidate for the title of 17ᵗʰ Karmapa, to whom he had given the name Trinley Thaye Dorje. Very shortly afterwards, the latter's enthronement ceremony took place in the Karmapa International Buddhist Institute in Delhi, a place which had been constructed in fulfilment of the 16ᵗʰ's wishes. It seems that some supporters of Situ Rinpoche attempted, unsuccessfully, to storm the Institute and so prevent the enthronement taking place.

At the end of my time in Poland, I flew to Stuttgart. There, I taught Rangjung Dorje's *Showing the Essence of the Tathagata* together with Jamgon Kongtrul's commentary, entitled *Clarifying the Thought of Rangjung*. The third and final leg of my trip was to Bulgaria: it was my fourth visit. On this occasion, some days of teachings had been arranged in a villa on the slopes of Mount Vitosha, just outside Sofia. About a dozen people, who had already taken refuge, attended my teaching on Tsarchen Losal Gyamtso's commentary on the *Fifty Verses on the Lama*. At the conclusion, I gave the initiation of Vajrasattva Heruka.

In Sofia itself, I gave a public talk, followed by several days of teaching on Tokme Zangpo's *Thirty-Seven Practices of a Buddha's Child*. It was during this time that I finally stumbled upon the sunny side of love, when I developed a romantic connection with my translator, Albena Ilieva. As it says in the tantras that one must rely on a consort who is capable of maintaining the requisite vows and pledges, the dakinis and dharma-protectors must have been involved. Albena was from a family in the small city of Dobrich, in the east of the country. After leaving school, she had studied Philology at Sofia University, and now worked for a publishing house there. Although she had already been practising the sadhanas of Chenrezi and Tara following my previous visits, she would later go on to accomplish Konchok Chindu and Vajrayogini.

The following month, back in England and with a sense that things had changed, I gave the Vajrasattva Heruka initiation again and also taught on *Parting from the Four Attachments*. Just after this, I made a trip to Karma Ling in Savoie to participate in a conference for European dharma teachers, hosted by Lama Denys. It was pleasant to see old friends and acquaintances again but I have to admit that the theme of the conference seemed to elude me.

Karma Thinley Rinpoche returned to Britain in August. For the first week, he stayed in my home in order to continue to bestow the *One Hundred Sadhanas of Bari Lotsava*. During these seven days, Rinpoche managed to give thirty-nine further initiations from the collection, including those for Chenrezi, and the three goddesses – Tara, Marichi and Prajna Paramita. At the beginning of the second week, we transferred to Liverpool. Many students came there to receive eight more initiations from *A Collection of Sadhanas*: Atisha's Protection Circle of Chenrezi, Bhikshuni Lakshmi's One Thousand-Armed Chenrezi and Five Dakinis of Chenrezi, Utsarya Vajrapani, Mahachakra Vajrapani, Shakyashribhadra's White and Green Taras and, finally, the initiation of Manjushri in connection with the 'Gangloma' praise. As always, extensive offerings were made to Rinpoche at the end of the teachings.

Within a few days of Rinpoche's departure for Toronto, I returned to Sofia. There, I continued with the teaching on the *Thirty-Seven Practices* before travelling to Varna once again to give some short teachings. Albena and I then flew to Poland. On this occasion, my itinerary took in not just Torun, but also Bydgocz and the city of Olsztyn in the north-east of the country. It was very cold up there; one could feel the wind blow in all the way from Lithuania. I gave the initiations of Chenrezi, Dzambhala and Atisha's Green Tara. Afterwards, we were shown the retreat-centre near Warsaw that was being constructed by Tenga Rinpoche's disciple, Lama Rinchen.

Among other important developments, 1994 also saw the influx of a number of Manchester University students into our community, such as Sam van Schaik, a circumstance which led to a strengthening of our work. The first area to benefit was Ganesha Press; I placed it under the direction of Adrian O'Sullivan and Paul Haddon, recent graduates in Philosophy. From this time onwards, there would be a steady stream of booklets, translations and commentaries, which would support our teaching programmes, particularly those of our 'seminaries'.

Actually, as long ago as 1975, Rinpoche had envisaged the creation of such a seminary, where the major textual works of the Kagyu and Sakya traditions could be studied. His intention had been that it should be named the Mikyo Dorje Institute in honour of the eponymous Karmapa. In fact, Rinpoche did establish such a seminary at that time in Toronto. However, he had been forced to abandon this project after a couple of years, and, although Rinpoche had hoped that a second seminary could be established in the United Kingdom, it had not proved possible.

By 1994, however, it seemed that a small-scale seminary programme might be viable in this country. Our plan was for several days of textual teaching every New Year, followed by organised study groups throughout the ensuing twelve months. Indeed, for the Sakya part of our community, a similar programme had already begun to take shape with Sonam Tsemo's *General Presentation of the Tantra Sets* at Changlochen. So, that New Year, we launched just such a seminary event of several days, consisting of teaching on the 3rd Karmapa's *Discriminating between Consciousness and Primordial Wisdom*. As in Germany, I used Rinpoche's own commentary to elucidate the root text. Around fifty people came to Liverpool for this beginning of the Mikyo Dorje seminary.

1995 was another year of travel, teaching and important visits. In Britain, I gave the initiation of Chenrezi-Mahamudra at Thinley Rinchen Ling. For Kagyu Dechen Dzong, our new centre, established by the hoteliers Howard and Tricia Quinn in the lovely Yorkshire town of Harrogate, I gave the initiation of Milarepa. Finally, at New Year, I completed Rangjung Dorje's text at the seminary. My first major journey of that same year occurred at Easter, taking in Bulgaria, Poland and Germany. In

Bulgaria, I confined myself to Sofia but, in Poland, I was invited to Sczcecin in the north-west of the country for the first time. Before that, Torun was the venue for the initiation of Konchok Chindu.

In May, Sakya Thinley Rinchen Ling was honoured by the visit of Her Eminence Jetsun Kushog, Chime Luding, the sister of H.H. Sakya Trizin and one of the foremost teachers of the Sakya tradition. Though several years older than her brother, she had trained alongside him in Tibet. Now the mother of four grown-up children, she has resided for many years in Vancouver with her husband, Sey Kushog. During her days with us, Jetsun Kushog gave a well-attended public talk in Bristol, insisting in her understated way that women do not require any special female dharma, as Lord Buddha intended his teaching to be for men and women equally. While she was with us, she also bestowed the initiations of two wisdom deities – White Saraswati from the lineage of the fourteenth-century polymath, Bodong Cholay Namgyal, and Bari Lotsava's Manjushri Arapatsana.

Within a few weeks, her visit was followed by that of His Holiness himself. Many people, both Buddhist and non-Buddhist, came to his public teaching in Bristol this time. His Holiness gave the initiation of Green Tara from the lineage of Atisha in addition to the initiation of Za'i Yum Chenmo (the Great Mother of the Planets). This deity, who is particularly associated with His Holiness's own Khon family lineage, counters malign astrological influences.

A month or so later, I was in France. At our meeting the previous year, Lama Denys had asked me to teach *Discriminating between Consciousness and Primordial Wisdom* at his summer school. Thus, in July, I made a trip to Savoie to fulfil this commitment. Although the school was not particularly well-attended, it allowed me to meet up with Khenpo Tsultrim Gyamtso, who was also teaching there. He had visited us in Manchester a couple of times in the 1980s but I hadn't seen him since then.

Once my duties at the summer school were at an end, I travelled to Changlochen. There, I continued with Sonam Tsemo's *General Presentation of the Tantra Sets* and gave the initiation of White Manjushri according to the lineage of Mati Panchen, which had been disseminated in Tibet by the eminent Kashmiri master Shayashribhadra in the thirteenth century. Although he had transmitted this particular cycle to his Kagyu disciple Trophu Lotsava, many of Shakyashri's teachings, such as the initiations of White and Green Tara, both of which I had received from Karma Thinley Rinpoche, passed through his other major Tibetan disciple, Sakya Pandita.

At the end of August, Rinpoche returned from Nepal. For the first week of his visit, he stayed with me again to continue bestowing the *One Hundred Sadhanas of Bari*; during this time, Rinpoche completed a further twenty-three initiations from this collection. Among these initiations were those of the Pancharaksha goddesses, whose protective rituals are very popular among Newar Buddhists, and various forms of the 'magnetising' goddess Kurukulla.

Subsequently, in Liverpool, Rinpoche gave five more initiations from *A Collection of Sadhanas*: Black Dzamb-hala; Dampa Sangye's Manjushri Lion Speech; Manjushri Namasamgiti; Hayagriva, Vajrapani and Garuda in a single initiation; and, finally, the initiation of the combined three long-life deities – Amitayus, White Tara and Namgyalma.

By the end of this fortnight, Rinpoche was quite tired. Now in his mid-sixties, he had been journeying back and forth to Nepal for seven years. However, he was already planning further trips. His aim was to construct a temple and residence in Shardar, close to his birthplace in the province of Nangchen. However, before work on that project could start, Rinpoche gave his blessing to developments closer to home. As a consequence, immediately following his departure, Sakya Thinley Rinchen Ling purchased a large house in the St. Andrew's area of Bristol. With this development, Bristol became our key centre for the next few years, especially after the near-collapse in 1997 of Shedrup Ling in Liverpool, brought about largely by difficulties within the administration there.

If 1995 was busy, the following year, by contrast, was rather quiet. In Bristol, my teaching programme, throughout both this and the subsequent year, was based on Patrul Rinpoche's *Words of My Perfect Master*. Many people came to receive this text, the only occasion on which I have given a teaching from outside of the Sakya tradition there. In addition to this, I visited Karma Lodro Ling twice to complete Rangjung Dorje's text, as well as teaching in Torun and Sczcecin. At the end of the year, the now annual Mikyo Dorje seminary took place. The main teaching was the first half of Rangjung Dorje's *Showing the Essence of the Tathagata*, together with its commentary by Jamgon Kongtrul.

Before my autumn visit to Poland and Germany, I had attended a second European Dharma Teachers' Conference. It had been held in the Kamalashila Institute, a Kagyu centre located in the flat German countryside to the west of Bonn. As I looked around the gathering of well-meaning people there, I wondered if a Buddhist commissariat was taking shape. It certainly appeared that many attending believed themselves to possess the necessary stature to design the future of Buddhism. It was not a pleasing prospect, but I was at least happy to meet up with such people as Dr Alex Berzin, the American Gelug scholar, whom I knew and respected. I can't remember whether or not I said anything at this gathering. Probably I didn't. After all, I'm no kind of prophet; I just know what I know.

What was particularly noticeable about this meeting, and other similar ones that I've attended over the years, is just how detached from the ongoing traditions of Asian dharma many of the participants seem to be. Rather than view themselves as apprentices within a particular tradition, whose authority to teach is entirely dependent on their own masters, they clearly regard themselves as self-sufficient authorities. What is more, they intend to bring about a 'Buddhist Reformation' in line with their predictable cultural predilections. This phenomenon has only worsened over the last two decades, and is even more marked in the United States than Europe. Unfortunately, most Asian Buddhists are unaware of this trend; only a few have any sense of just how far from the shore of the prior tradition much Western Buddhism is drifting – not so much in outer appearance, which is ultimately trivial, but in its abandonment or ignorance of core teachings.

I returned to Poland in the following spring of 1997 to teach Nagarjuna's *Letter to a Friend* in Torun and to begin teaching Patrul Rinpoche's *Words of my Perfect Master* in Sczcecin. This teaching had been requested by Ven. Kanzen, a Polish Soto Zen priest, who ran the Buddhist Mission in that city. Coincidentally, I also began to teach

Patrul Rinpoche's work at Karma Lodro Ling around this time. That same spring back in England, I taught Dharmarakshita's *Wheel of Sharp Weapons*, a famous exposition of *Mind-Training* preserved in the Kadam tradition and part of the *One Hundred Mind-Trainings Collection* that Rinpoche had given me in Toronto. Dharmarakshita had been one of the three masters, alongside Dharmakirti and Maitriyogin, to transmit *Mind-Training* teachings to Atisha, before the latter brought them to Tibet.

August saw us return to Changlochen for what was, in those days, a biennial seminary. There I continued with Sonam Tsemo's *General Presentation of the Tantra Sets*, and gave the initiation of Shakyashribhadra's Green Tara. A month later, Rinpoche stopped over in London for a couple of days on his way back to Toronto. I received the reading-transmission for Karma Chakme's celebrated *Union of Mahamudra and Great Perfection* from him, a transmission that I had wanted to obtain for many years, having heard so much about this text from various lamas. Rinpoche also gave the transmission for Karma Chakme's notes on *The Great Vajradhara Prayer*.

Just after Rinpoche's fleeting visit, I travelled to our group in Exeter, where I gave the initiation of Green Tara from the lineage of Atisha and taught Ngawang Lekpa's *Nectar of Good Fortune*. The year ended with the second half of *Showing the Essence of the Tathagata* at the Mikyo Dorje seminary, which had now relocated from Liverpool to Manchester.

You could call 1998 an eventful year. In January, I bestowed the initiation of Sakya Pandita in Bristol. Two months later, I flew with Albena to Kathmandu to await Rinpoche's imminent arrival from Toronto. His brother, the lay-tantrika Konchok Gyalpo, a skilled flautist with a keen appreciation of female pulchritude, was already installed in the nunnery, together with several other members of Rinpoche's family. Thus it was that a large party greeted Rinpoche on his arrival at the airport.

Our stay in Legshay Ling provided a chance for Rinpoche to give me the final six initiations of the *One-Hundred Sadhanas of Bari*. As Bari Lotsava had brought together sadhanas from all four classes of tantras and for all four categories of 'mundane' accomplishments – pacifying, increasing, magnetising and wrathful – the collection was an extraordinary resource and Rinpoche urged me to employ it for the benefit of others.

Before I left Kathmandu, Rinpoche also made the time to give me the reading-transmissions for Shantarakshita's *Ornament of Madhyamaka,* a work which expounds a synthesis of Yogachara and Madhyamaka viewpoints, and his own recently composed *Telescope of Wisdom*, a commentary on Nagarjuna's *Letter to a Friend*. At the end of this period of teaching, I flew to Germany to continue with the *Words of My Perfect Master*.

By 1998, the number of committed practitioners belonging to our Sakya and Kagyu community had almost doubled from what it had been five years earlier. Outside of this circle of serious practice, there were also many other people who attended our classes in Bristol, Manchester, Harrogate and elsewhere. Some attended once, some stayed for longer, and some gained real contemplative experience, thus demonstrating that the Vajrayana works in the West.

It seems that such distinct levels of engagement are typical of all dharma communities in the West. Nevertheless, it is certain that to progress along the Vajrayana path one must be properly educated in the vows and pledges intrinsic to the tantric teachings. Without the support of these ethical disciplines and perspectives, any efforts to gain accomplishment through Vajrayana practice will be in vain. Consequently, to meet this educational need, I have taught the *Fifty Verses* and related works frequently over the years.

In August of that year, I made a brief retreat on Vajrayogini, and then, a few weeks later, we were plunged into the maelstrom of activity engendered by H.H. Sakya Trizin's sixth visit. On this occasion he was accompanied by his elder son, Ratna Vajra Rinpoche, who had just finished his education at Sakya College in Rajpur. In the first two days of this visit, His Holiness bestowed the major initiation of the Mahayoga deity, Vajrakilaya, and one hundred and fifty students gathered in Bristol to receive this highly prized teaching. It had been given by Padmasambhava to Nagarakshita from the aristocratic Khon family in the late eighth century and its unbroken oral transmission had been preserved exclusively in the Sakya tradition.

Subsequently, His Holiness gave an extensive teaching on *Parting from the Four Attachments*, which drew students from the local Gelug centre, as well as our own people. In some free time, His Holiness bestowed upon me the reading-transmissions for the brief and extensive practices of Vajrakilaya composed by Sachen Kunga Lodro and Sakya Lotsava Jamyang Dorje respectively. I had accomplished Chogyur Lingpa's *Secret Drop Vajrakilaya* in the late 1970s, and so it was useful now to amplify my understanding a little with these more detailed presentations of Kilaya practice from the oral transmission lineage.

The second part of His Holiness's programme took place at Sakya Goshak Choling, our group in Birmingham. There, he gave a talk attended by the general public and members of the city's various Buddhist groups. His Holiness also found the time to give our students the initiation of Vajrapani Bhutadamara to dispel obstacles. Following His Holiness's visit, I began to teach Jetsun Drakpa Gyaltsen's *Dispelling Error*, his major work on the Vajrayana vows and pledges, in Thinley Rinchen Ling. Then, in April, I travelled again to Karma Lodro Ling to continue with the *Words of My Perfect Master*. During this visit, a Karma-Kagyu group located in the Swabisch Alb, south of Stuttgart, requested me to give teachings. The sangha there was under the direction of Lama Ole Nyidahl. To oblige them, I gave a talk on the *Four Seals*.

After my return from Germany, a long period of legal disentanglement from my first marriage finally came to an end. Albena and I were then able to marry in a small civil ceremony in Manchester, with just a couple of songs by Sinatra being played as celebration. Mr Frank did not let us down. Our honeymoon was then spent attending *A Midsummer Night's Dream* in Stratford-on-Avon.

Chapter Six
Keys of the Kingdom

After that date with the Fairy Queen, we flew into the future. It was a new era, and it began in Sofia, where I taught the *Fifty Verses on the Lama*, and gave the initiation of Chenrezi-Mahamudra to a small group of students. Travelling from there to Poland, I continued with the *Words of My Perfect Master* in Sczcecin and then, in Torun, I taught the *Fifty Verses on the Lama*.

Two weeks after this Polish trip, the biennial seminary in Changlochen took place. For this course and the subsequent courses of 2001 and 2003, the principal teaching would be Shantideva's *Entering the Conduct of a Bodhisattva*. I had taught it twice before in the 1980s, but there had been quite an influx of people since then, making it necessary to teach it again. At the end, I gave the same initiation of Manjushri that Rinpoche himself had bestowed some years earlier in Liverpool.

Although Rinpoche passed through England twice every year, it had been four years since his last extensive visit. Therefore, it was a particularly significant event when, that September, he gave the initiation of White Tara from Shakyashribhadra's lineage and that of Red Tara according to Jetsun Drakpa Gyaltsen, third of the five venerable masters of Sakya. Around one hundred and fifty people received these teachings in Thinley Rinchen Ling.

In the days following these initiations, Rinpoche gave me the reading-transmissions for a number of important cycles connected with particular empowerments that he had previously bestowed. Thus he gave me Jamgon Kongtrul's guiding instructions on the Four Kadam Deities, as well as all the texts relating to Mahachakra Vajrapani and Utsarya Vajrapani. Once they were concluded, he read the transmission for the cycles of Shakyashribhadra's White and Green Taras, as well as for Jetsun Drakpa's Red Tara. Finally, Rinpoche bestowed the transmissions for several other miscellaneous rituals of Tara upon me.

That same autumn, Theseus Verlag, a German publishing house, brought out my book, *Die Lehre Vom Glück*, a volume of introductory teachings translated by Andrea Liebers, a journalist and author from Heidelberg. This publication more or less coincided with my November visit to Germany. As on my preceding visit, I gave some teachings to the group in the Swabisch Alb, in addition to my normal duties at Karma Lodro Ling.

The year and the millennium then came to an end with the Mikyo Dorje seminary in Manchester, where I taught the third in the cycle of Kagyu Zhentong works, the *Correct Analysis of the Zhentong Madhyamaka System* composed by the 8th Karmapa himself. The course concluded with the initiation of Sangye Menla, which I had already given more than a dozen times. The sadhana for this practice was composed by the celebrated sixteenth-century master, Karma Chakme, who assisted Mingyur Dorje with the compilation of the Sky Dharma Treasures. Some people said that Karma Chakme was actually an emanation of Karmapa Mikyo Dorje. He was certainly very close to both the 6th Shamarpa, Chokyi Wangchuk, and the 10th Karmapa, Choying Dorje.

By this time, fourteen years had passed since the sale of the Kagyu Ling house in Manchester. It was a kind of rebirth, therefore, when in January 2000, the Kagyu Rime Ling Trust was able to purchase a detached property in South Manchester for Kagyu Ling. Although smaller in size than Sakya Thinley Rinchen Ling, this new house gave Kagyu Ling an appropriate basis for work. Jonathan MacAskill rapidly formed an able team with Geoff Ashmore, John Sainsbury and others to run the dharma classes, practice programme and essential administration.

In late March of that same year, Albena and I flew to Nepal with Rinpoche. There he bestowed upon me the first eleven initiations from the great Jetsun Kunga Drolchog's lineage of the initiations of the eighty-four siddhas. I would later receive the entire collection from H.H. Sakya Trizin. When this had concluded, Rinpoche's nuns performed an Amitayus ritual dedicated to my long life and that of Rinpoche himself. After the ritual had been concluded, the spring weather was fine enough to permit a two-day picnic in Legshay Ling's garden. It was sponsored by Rinpoche's uncle, Pon Namkha Dorje. Speeches were made, momos were eaten, and seemingly endless films of the Jyekundo horse-fair and other highlights of contemporary Tibetan culture were enjoyed by many.

During this same visit to Nepal, I became friendly

with Guru Lama, a Tsarpa monk and close disciple of Chogye Trichen Rinpoche. At that time, he was living with some mutual friends, Thubten and Tsering, in Bodha, and had recently launched Sachen International, an organisation dedicated to the publication of rare Sakyapa texts. I decided to sponsor a new edition of the collected teachings of Vajrayogini which he was planning; we would help with quite a few other publications, over the coming years.

Once back in England, I travelled to Bristol, where I gave a few days' teaching on the *Three Visions,* using the text composed by Ngawang Chodrak. In the following months, I gave the initiation of Amitabha in Manchester and that of Choling's Vajrasattva in Harrogate. That same autumn, I finished teaching the *Words of My Perfect Master* in Karma Lodro Ling and also taught *Parting from the Four Attachments* and gave the initiation of Chenrezi-Mahamudra to the group in Torun. Finally, at the Mikyo Dorje seminary, a new cycle of teachings began with the *Jewel Ornament of Liberation.*

2001 saw me give a number of different teachings. At Thinley Rinchen Ling, I taught Atisha's *Jewel Rosary of a Bodhisattva*, Geshe Langri Thangpa's *Eight Verses of Mind-Training* and bestowed the initiations of Manjushri Arapatsana and Namgyalma from the lineage of Bari Lotsava. In addition, for those new to Vajrayana practice, I taught the *Fifty Verses on the Lama*. However, I was less occupied at Kagyu Ling that year, just giving the initiation of Konchok Chindu in March and continuing with the *Jewel Ornament of Liberation*.

A couple of years earlier, Thorson's, a publishing division of Harper Collins, had commissioned me to write a book on Tibetan Buddhism for an introductory series on spiritual traditions. As requested, I tried to make it accessible for the modern reader. The book was published that spring under the title *Way of Tibetan Buddhism* and dedicated to His Holiness and Rinpoche, the latter having provided the foreword.

Following its publication, I visited Poland to give the initiation of Sakya Pandita in Torun and further teachings on the *Words of My Perfect Master* in Sczcecin. Then, in France, that August, I continued with *Entering the Conduct of a Bodhisattva*.

It was that same month that my academic career reached its end, after more than two decades. Thanks to the support provided by many dharma students, I was able to resign from my posts at the Manchester Metropolitan University and the University of Manchester. Of course, to be truthful, it had been a career into which I had just drifted but, despite the collapse in academic standards over the last few decades, I still see the profession itself as one worthy of respect, and feel considerable gratitude to my own teachers and professors. They all took seriously their duty to ensure the conservation of the inherited wisdom of human culture, to introduce successive generations to those treasures and to train them in the skills of analytical thinking and enquiry.

It was for exactly these reasons that dharma-masters of the past, such as Sakya Pandita, ensured that the great works of Indian arts and sciences were assimilated into Tibetan civilisation, alongside the dharma itself. Similarly, we should remember that it was eminent Christian thinkers, from Augustine to Aquinas, and the later scholars of the Renaissance, who preserved the best of pre-Christian Classical Civilization. Therefore I think that we Buddhists in the West need to adopt the same perspective in regard to the best in our own culture. It can support our dharma, since it embodies both beauty and a measure of wisdom. It need hardly be mentioned that a similar appreciation should be extended towards that which is life-enhancing in the fields of science and medicine.

Late that autumn, Albena and I flew to India to see His Holiness Sakya Trizin. It was a visit that I had been discussing with him for some time. We arrived in Rajpur on the 6th of December. While we were there, His Holiness bestowed upon us the initiations and transmissions for the two protector-deities known as Chitapati, the Sixteen Arhats according to the lineage of Atisha and the White and Red Saraswatis of the Bodong lineage.

All four initiations took place in His Holiness's personal shrine room. On a free day between teachings, we visited Sakya College. His Holiness had invited us to attend the ceremony marking the opening of a three-week period of debate and discussion carried out by the College's students. Sakya College itself was situated a couple of miles from His Holiness's palace and Sakya Centre.

Apart from receiving teachings from His Holiness, a second purpose for the trip was to discuss his next visit to England. Happily, we were able to make a detailed programme for his time in Bristol and Manchester the following year. Very pleased to have accomplished this and to have spent time with His Holiness, we returned to England in good time for the Mikyo Dorje seminary.

Thanks to the blessings of my lamas, I was able to complete four weeks of retreat on Vajrayogini in 2002. Various auspicious signs occurred during these weeks, including a dream in which I saw Dilgo Khyentse Rinpoche again after twenty-six years. In the dream, I was in Nepal, and Khyentse Rinpoche was standing on the other bank of a river. He urged me to cross the flood but I held back, telling him that I did not possess all six million, four hundred thousand verses of the Great Perfection. To this, Khyentse Rinpoche replied: 'What you have is enough'. At this, I felt relieved and happy and waded into the water.

In March, Karma Thinley Rinpoche visited us for five days on the way to Nepal. Staying with us in Manchester, he gave me the reading-transmission for Patrul Rinpoche's *Virtuous in the Beginning, Middle and End*, a beautiful work on combining meditation on the deity Chenrezi with the perspective of the Great Perfection. Apart from giving this transmission and blessing Kagyu Ling's new house, Rinpoche's principal activity during his stay was his bestowal of the initiation of Vajravarahi on members of our dharma-community. It was the second time that he had given it for Kagyu Ling. The day after this major empowerment, Rinpoche flew on to Nepal for his annual residency in Legshay Ling.

The following month, we visited Zurich at the request of Andrew and Dolma Gutmann, who had settled there a couple of years earlier. Much of the time was taken up by discussions about the new administrative structure for the community, which Andrew was overseeing. Tony Lister and Angela Brady were taking up new posts in the administration, as were Paul Haddon and my eldest daughter Rosalind, who would marry later that year. She had just completed her degree in Classics at Oxford.

Our stay in Switzerland was followed by visits both to Sofia, where I gave the Manjushri Arapatsana initiation, and to Sczcecin, where I finished teaching the *Words of My Perfect Master* and gave the initiation of the longevity goddess, Namgyalma. On the way to Poland, we had stopped in Berlin to have dinner with H.H. Sakya Trizin. He was visiting the city for two days as part of his tour of Europe.

It was the last time we would go to Poland for many years. I had come to the conclusion that the conditions were not propitious. The dharma there was decided by other voices, and there was not much that I could usefully contribute at that time. So I decided that I should wait and see what happened in the future. Sometimes a man's got to know his limitations.

A few months later, His Holiness, with his younger son, Gyana Vajra Rinpoche, arrived on his seventh visit to Sakya Thinley Rinchen Ling. The first full day of His Holiness's programme, 28th October, was taken up with Chogyal Phakpa's *Letter of Instructions to Kublai Khan*, a lucid summation of moral discipline, meditation and wisdom. People from many dharma-organisations attended this event. Over the next two days, His Holiness bestowed the initiation of Chakrasamvara from the lineage of Krishnacharya on one hundred and sixty students from our community, together with a few people from other Sakya groups. This major empowerment was followed by that of Vajrayogini Naro Khechari.

His Holiness's activity seemed boundless. In Manchester he bestowed the initiations of Vajrapani Mahachakra and White Manjushri, while privately giving me the reading-transmissions for the entire cycle of White Manjushri, as well as Khyentse Wangpo's sadhana of Chakrasamvara. Finally, before His Holiness's departure, we made plans for our next trip to Rajpur.

The year ended with the third session of the *Jewel Ornament of Liberation* at the Mikyo Dorje seminary. Then, early in 2003, I gave the initiations of White and Green Tara, both from Shakyashribhadra's lineage, at Thinley Rinchen Ling. Later on, I also gave the initiations of Maitreya and Black Dzambala from the *One-Hundred Sadhanas of Bari* there. In the course of that same year, I was able to accomplish a further three weeks of retreat on Vajrayogini and a week on White Tara.

In my Vajrayogini retreat, I had a dream in which I was sailing in a ship, together with His Holiness and Rinpoche. My wife was also there, and, towards the back of the boat, I spied some shadowy figures, who might have been two or three poets or musicians, whose work I have long admired. I had the sense that we had embarked on this voyage a long time before. Although the shore, for which we had set out, was not yet in sight, I knew that we were moving towards it. Perhaps we were sailing for Ithaca, or maybe it was Byzantium. Either way, it was clear to me that the boat had crossed the mid-point of its voyage.

That year, Rinpoche had invited us to join him on his annual visit to Legshay Ling. We flew out with him from London on the 22nd of March to find that many of Rinpoche's relatives, including Jedrung Rinpoche and Zangpo Rinpoche, were staying in the nunnery. Outside, the atmosphere in Kathmandu itself was peaceful, thanks to the cease-fire that had been negotiated between the government and the Maoist terrorist group which, at that point, controlled one half of the country. After two weeks we returned to England, while Rinpoche journeyed to Nangchen.

Two months after this trip to Nepal, I gave the initiation of Namgyalma in Zurich. While there, I dreamed that we were travelling in India. My 'zen' had frayed and was being repaired by His Holiness. Next to him, as he worked, there was a life-size statue of Saraswati, goddess of wisdom. Suddenly, the deity came alive and began to talk.

In the event, the actual journey prefigured by this dream began on 20th October, when, accompanied by Carl Rogers and David Armstrong, we flew to Delhi. After a very brief stop-over there, we arrived in Rajpur three days later. I had already discussed the particular teachings to be given with His Holiness, and so, two days after our arrival, he bestowed the major initiation of Akshobyavajra-Guhyasamaja according to the lineage of Nagarjuna, together with the reading-transmission for the sadhana composed by Sachen Kunga Lodro in the eighteenth century. This initiation and the subsequent series took place in the great lhakhang of Shri Sakya Centre itself, in order to accommodate the many monks and nuns who wished to receive these rare teachings that I had requested. His Holiness's family also attended this and the following initiations.

According to tradition, the Guhyasamaja tantra was the first tantra to be bestowed by the Buddha, when he gave it in response to a request by King Indrabhuti from Oddiyana. So, it has a particular significance to all followers of the Vajrayana. On the first night of the initiation, I dreamed of walking along a mountainside. Shimmering rainbow lights filled the sky, surrounding a great cave. I looked inside and saw Guru Padmasambhava. Concentric rainbow circles were pouring endlessly from him and pervading the entire world. I was filled with an indescribable joy that remained with me throughout the succeeding days.

Once the two days of the Guhyasamaja initiation were over, His Holiness began to give the set of initiations known as the *One-Hundred Sadhanas of Narthang*

(Narthang Gyatsa). These thirty-four initiations and their related sadhanas, brought to Tibet by Atisha, had been collected together in the thirteenth century by Chim Namkha Drak, abbot of the influential Kadam monastery of Narthang. Having subsequently passed through a line of Kadam and Gelug masters, the collection had then entered the Sakya tradition in the seventeenth century with the polymath Zhuchen Tsultrim Rinchen in Dege. His Holiness himself had obtained it when he received the entirety of *A Collection of Sadhanas* from his guru, Ngawang Lodro Tenzin Nyingpo.

Each day His Holiness gave several initiations, until he had completed the collection. On the last night, I dreamed that I was in the middle of a great hall. Above and all around me innumerable Buddhas were performing a ceremony of enthronement. As I lifted up my head, I understood that I had been crowned, and in my hand was a sword, which I now held aloft. As I did so, the deities proclaimed my secret name to me.

To close this extraordinary sequence of teachings, His Holiness bestowed the major yoga tantra initiation of Sarvavid Vairochana, a cycle which is very frequently performed for the deceased. At the end of the many days of initiations, I made extensive offerings and sponsored the monastic community to make prayers for His Holiness's long life. Two days later I received some parting instructions and the reading-transmission for Ngorchen Kunga Zangpo's sadhana of Sarvavid from His Holiness and we returned to England, arriving home on the 5th of November.

A few nights later, after I had been hesitating once again about whether to continue writing this account, I dreamed that His Holiness, Rinpoche and Vajrayogini appeared together, urging me to persevere with the task.

Chapter Seven
Maps of the Interior

By this time in 2004, many years had passed since the wave of dharma that had arrived on our shores in the late 1960s and early 1970s. Centres had been established, masters had shown up, teachings had been given, and some practice had been done. Yet now the moment for dharma seemed to have gone, and the cultural focus appeared to have shifted elsewhere. Of course, it wasn't just Buddhism that was affected. The spiritual life, in all its serious traditional forms, had faded in fashionability.

It was quite another story, however, when it came to secularised spirituality in the form of phenomena like yoga and 'mindfulness'. They were proliferating rapidly in every nook and cranny, but their success owed much to their distance from their original sources. Thus, in general, the new atmosphere appeared to be as resolutely hostile to religion as it was, nominally at least, pro-science. It was an atmosphere that had been building since the 1980s.

It cannot be denied that religious organisations had contributed to their own eclipse through the regular occurrence of scandals. While some such scandals were bogus, ginned up for political advantage, personal revenge or financial gain, many, regrettably, were not. Thus, some of the reputational advantages that Buddhism had enjoyed, thirty years earlier, by reason of its intellectual depth, its authentically saintly exemplars, its non-theistic spirituality and its very newness on the Western scene, had now been squandered. Nevertheless, the dharma itself, as always, remains pure and powerful.

As for our dharma world, although the next few years would bring some major developments, they began quietly enough. In that year of 2004, I gave the initiations of Yellow Vasudhara and Sitatapatra from Bari Lotsava, as well as Chenrezi-Mahamudra and Gonkar, all in Bristol. In Kagyu Ling, meanwhile, I taught Jamgon Kongtrul's commentary on the *Seven Points of Mind-Training*, followed by another of his most influential works, the commentary on Maitreya's *Supreme Continuity*, entitled *The Lion's Roar*. I also managed to give a teaching in Harrogate on Chogyur Dechen Lingpa's text *Liberation by Hearing in the Bardo*, which connects the experience of the intermediate state between death and rebirth with the practice of the Great Perfection. It is a teaching that I had received from Khamtrul Rinpoche, many years previously.

In the spring-time, Andrew and Dolma Gutmann invited me to teach *The Fifty Verses on the Lama*, at a course held in the mountains outside Zurich. Afterwards, we spent a little time in the city itself, a place made attractive by its beautiful lake. You could feel that there was a certain seriousness about money and shopping in the air. Consequently, the times when the Protestant Reformer Ulrich Zwingli had personally supervised the drowning of a few

Anabaptists in the sixteenth century seemed long-gone. It was quite some time too since Mr Joyce was squinting at the waitresses and talking in tongues, while Lenin sat at the next table in the Café Odéon, waiting for a train to St Petersburg. The Odéon is still doing good business, but nobody seemed to be writing a new version of *Ulysses*, or planning a revolution, when we stopped in for coffee.

On our last day there, we took a boat-trip on Zurich See. A few miles down the lake is Bollingen, former home of C.G. Jung, a modern seer 'with a wicked pack of cards'. As we sailed by it, I thought of him and how, without entirely intending to do so, he had perhaps prepared some ground for dharma in the West.

Three months later, in July, our daughter Katharina was born, and H.H. Sakya Trizin sent her the dharma-name Ngawang Chödrön. It was just after this that we left Manchester to settle in London. We had found an apartment in Bayswater, an area that I had known quite well some thirty years previously. It was situated in a garden square, five minutes away from Kensington Gardens. Despite my strong roots in Manchester, it seemed like the right time to make this move. For me, London was the city of Keats and Blake, who had seen angels in Peckham. I remembered that in 1970 we'd seen some wonders in Ladbroke Grove, too.

Having settled in there, we travelled to Rajpur in January, to spend some time with H.H. Sakya Trizin. Although she was only six months old, Katharina came with us in order to receive a long-life blessing from His Holiness in the Phodrang. After this blessing, His Holiness bestowed the major initiation of Vajrabhairava and the thirteen Vetalis from the lineage of Rwa Lotsava. This twelfth-century yogin and translator had been involved in the transmission of anuttara tantra cycles such as Kalachakra, Yamantaka and Vajrabhairava, the wrathful form of Manjushri.

Although he was well-known for his meditative accomplishment in these systems, Rwa Lotsava had enjoyed rather troubled relationships with a number of other contemporary masters, including Marpa's son, Darma Dode. Nevertheless, this particular lineage of Vajrabhairava had been preserved in the Tsar branch of Sakya. Although Vajrabhairava is classed as father-line anuttara tantra like Guhyasamaja, it is concerned with the transformation of the disturbing emotion of hatred, whereas the latter focusses on the transformation of desire.

In addition to this major initiation, His Holiness also gave the initiations of Vajrapani from the Drozang lineage and Guru Drakmar from the lineage of the twelfth-century 'treasure-revealer', Nyangral Nyima Ozer. All these took place in Sakya Centre itself and were attended by the ordained sangha of monks and nuns. However, the initiation of the major form of Kurukulla from the *Thirteen Golden Dharmas* was restricted to a few close disciples and members of the Phodrang. Immediately after receiving the initiation of this goddess, we left for England.

Back in Europe, my own duties were quite varied that year. In Bristol, I gave the initiations of the two goddesses, Prajnaparamita and Namgyalma, from Bari Lotsava's collection, as well as the initiation of Manjushri based upon the 'Gangloma' prayer and that of Sakya Pandita. In Manchester, I taught the *Four Dharmas of Gampopa* and gave the initiation of Konchog Chindu, while in Harrogate I gave the initiation of Amitayus from the Taklung Kagyu tradition.

For the third year in succession, we visited Zurich. On this occasion, I gave the initiation of Wishfulfilling-Wheel White Tara, together with the guiding instructions composed by Ngawang Legdrup, one of Jamyang Khyentse Wangpo's masters. It was the first time that I had given this transmission, which I had received from Phende Rinpoche in 1987. On this same trip, we stopped over in Stuttgart, where, with the assistance of Wolfgang and Hilde Staufner, we launched the new centre, Sakya Dechen Ling, one of the few Sakya centres in Germany.

Sometimes things happen when you least expect them, and so it was with our meeting with His Holiness the 17th Karmapa. In fact, I had long wanted to see him but political realities had made it difficult. Nonetheless, back in 1994, when Karmapa, Trinley Thaye Dorje, was brought to India from Lhasa by Shamar Rinpoche, my knowledge that the latter had been assisted by Chogye Tri Rinpoche made me confident that this was the actual incarnation.

However, it was evident that the majority of Tibetans had accepted the declarations of Situ Rinpoche and the Ganden Phodrang, and, every so often, we were made aware of the consequences of stepping out of line on this issue. In a situation where the pressure to conform was strong, I had been careful not to push in any direction.

The stimulus that changed this came suddenly. While I was in Exeter to give the Green Tara initiation from the lineage of Atisha, I was contacted by an emissary from the Diamond Way, asking if I would be interested in meeting privately with H.H. the 17th Karmapa, Trinley Thaye Dorje, on his forthcoming trip to England, that summer of 2005.

It was quite a question, but it so happened that Rinpoche was in Nangchen, outside of the range of

communication, and thus I had to make the decision
unaided. A week or so later, Albena and I set out for an
address in South London, where this secret meeting was
to take place. His Holiness was twenty-two years old,
and seemed very happy to meet us. He was reflective in
his demeanour, with a gentle strength that was completely unforced and a wonderfully kind sense of humour. As with his predecessor, it was clear that he was
not an ordinary being or even an ordinary lama. It felt
like we were going to get to know each other very well
over the coming years. Before leaving, we resolved with
His Holiness to meet again on his next trip to Europe.

Thirty years earlier, Rinpoche had taught Nagarjuna's
Letter to a Friend at Kagyu Ling. Of course, since that time,
he had composed his own commentary, *The Telescope of
Wisdom*, which I had received from him in Nepal. So,
in 2006, I made this new commentary the principal
focus of my teaching at Sakya Centre in Bristol. Later, I
would teach it again, in both Manchester and Stuttgart,
and Ganesha Press would publish a translation of it by
Adrian O'Sullivan. As for our Kagyu centres, I gave the
initiation of Marpa, and taught some songs of Milarepa,
and gave the Sky Dharma treasure initiation of Chenrezi
and the initiation of Green Tara from Chogyur Lingpa.

2006 was also the year we launched our new centre,
Sakya Dechen Ling, in London. It would be a few years
before we could actually purchase a permanent place in
Notting Hill, but, that May, I taught Chogyal Phakpa's
Instructions to the Emperor, which His Holiness had
taught four years earlier. The new centre was a fulfilment of Karma Thinley Rinpoche's long-expressed wish
for a London centre, a project on which Steve Mulligan
had worked for many years.

This year, as in all other years, Rinpoche made his usual stop-overs with us, on the way to and from Nepal. This made it possible for me to receive the transmission for Jamgon Kongtrul's commentary on Atisha's influential *Lamp of the Path of Enlightenment*. Atisha's root-text had been the very first work belonging to the Graduated Path genre composed in Tibet and thus a model both for Sakya Pandita's *Elucidating the Thought of the Sage* and Gampopa's *Jewel Ornament*. Rinpoche had given me the root-text some thirty years earlier. Immediately on his departure, I made a Vajrayogini retreat, my first since our youngest daughter had been born.

In April, accompanied by Jonathan from Kagyu Ling, I visited Japan, at the invitation of Nembutsu-shu, a Pure Land Buddhist Organisation. This highly dedicated and energetic group had been the prime movers behind four World Buddhist Summits in the previous decade. I had been invited at the suggestion of Lama Denys from France. The purpose of the visit was to discuss the possibility that I attend the Summit in the future as the representative (or 'supreme Buddhist leader' as they flatteringly but inaccurately styled it) from the U.K. It appeared that the Summit organisers were seeking to extend the number of countries represented.

We were hosted with an almost overwhelming solicitude, being given a seven-day sight-seeing trip of several cities – Osaka, Kyoto, Kobe, Fukuoka and Hiroshima – the last a lonely reminder of the suffering that we humans visit upon each other. The temples that Nembutsu-shu had established in these cities were exquisite, not least the Royal Grand Hall of Buddhism complex, close to Kobe City, which serves as their headquarters. It is probably the nearest approximation to Amitabha's realm of Sukhavati that could be constructed in this world. As for Japan itself, although evidence of the country's secularisation and estrangement from dharma is undeniable and depressing, I couldn't help but feel that Buddha's teachings are still present in some way, just waiting to be summoned back to life.

One of our more memorable encounters took place in a Shinto temple, where we were able to talk for some time with the resident officiant. This impressive and thoughtful master revealed that, contrary to my presuppositions, he and other Shinto practitioners were also followers of the dharma. It seems that the notion of a separation between the two traditions was something of a distortion, fostered partly by recent Japanese politics and partly by American policy during the post-war occupation. His temple was dedicated to a particular local female kami and felt like a genuine place of power.

In fact, wherever we travelled in Japan, I had the sense that the local deities or 'kami' still dwelt in each stream and hill. It reminded me that such powerful samsaric beings have always been present in every landscape and every nation, merely being depicted in varying ways according to culture. You can sense them in many places in Britain if your mind is quiet: places like Castlerigg Stone Circle in the Lake District, or those associated with our once and future king, a man only temporarily laid low by betrayal. Unfortunately, we are too rushed to notice them, and thus have forgotten their existence, much to our own impoverishment. They should not be neglected.

I made three foreign trips to teach that year: Sofia to give Yellow Dzambala, Stuttgart to give Green Tara, and, finally, to our French centre, Sakya Changlochen Ling. This had been extensively rebuilt under the direction of its chief administrator, David Armstrong, a process that would continue in the coming years. In Changlochen, I gave a week of teaching based on my book *Rain of Clarity: The Stages of the Path in the Sakya Tradition*. I had composed this new work over the past year and both H.H. Sakya Trizin and Karma Thinley Rinpoche had contributed forewords to it. Ganesha Press brought it out in the U.K. and it was later published in translation by different publishing companies in Spain, France and Germany. It was short but not simple.

2006 also saw our first trip to California. We had received an invitation from one of my students, Laura Rubio, whose family owned a holiday villa in La Jolla, as well as from the photographer Ed Heckerman and his wife Simone in Santa Monica. Laura had been in Manchester for several years, carrying out research for her Ph.D. at the University of Manchester, and had now returned to Mexico City. There she was teaching in a private university, and was in the process of founding our centre, Sakya Dolma Ling.

Our U.S. trip began that May in a disappointingly chilly San Francisco, where we stayed in the Omni Hotel, close to the Transamerica building and on the edge of China Town. In the other direction, about fifteen minutes away, lay Union Square and the smart shops. San Francisco might have been unseasonably cold but it was full of meaning for me. In one supermarket, down near the Embarcadero, I thought that I saw Allen Ginsberg among the vegetables – just as, in a similar illumination, he had imagined glimpsing Walt Whitman, some fifty years earlier. Later, walking around North Beach, taking in the Italianate buildings and Gregory Corso's Coit tower, I recalled those times, when the Buddha's name was invoked amidst the howls and bebop prosody of those searching for beatitude. Lawrence Ferlinghetti was in the City Lights Bookshop the day we called in, but I didn't want to disturb him.

At the end of our time in San Francisco, we wove our way down the Pacific Coastal Highway to a somewhat warmer Los Angeles. It was a two-day trip down the P.C.H., by turns exhilarating, perilous and savage. Big Sur was quite fog-bound and unearthly, and, as we drove through it, crossing Bixby Canyon, I remembered Kerouac sinking into the waves there in the terrible sadness and disillusionment of samsara.

Once in L.A. we settled in the Viceroy Hotel by the sea in Santa Monica. It was a lively place, but we also enjoyed exploring the roads leading back from the beach, like Wilshire Boulevard. When we were north of Montana, I was sure that I saw Philip Marlowe paying a call to a Spanish-style house owned by a wealthy family. There was a Mexican gardener watering the manicured lawn, while one of the daughters was getting drunk by the pool in the back. The last I heard, the gardener was still there, but the blonde had run off with some elegantly wasted guy called Terry. She met him in The Ivy on The Shore.

After a couple of days looking round, I gave a teaching on a short text by Patrul Rinpoche to the members of the Yeshe Nyingpo centre. It had been founded by Dudjom Rinpoche back in the 1980s, and Acharya Ed had been appointed its director, after his return from Switzerland with Simone. Although I didn't foresee it, out of this small event a long-term involvement with L.A. was born.

It was a few months after this memorable first trip to the U.S. that the major dharma event of this year took place with H.H. Sakya Trizin. It happened in Pedreguer, southern Spain, where a centre named Fundación Sakya had been established through the sponsorship of a local businessman. It is set on the side of a cliff, some ten miles back from the Mediterranean, and surrounded, rather incongruously, by a housing development, populated by expatriates from northern lands.

There, for over thirty days, His Holiness gave the rarely bestowed guiding instructions on Vajrayogini from the teachings of Jamyang Khyentse Wangpo. In length, this is twice the size of the guiding instructions by Khyentse Wangchuk that I had received from Phende Rinpoche back in the early 1980s. His Holiness himself had received it from the late Dezhung Rinpoche. It was a wonderful opportunity to obtain such detailed instructions. We took David, Carl and Liz from Bristol as assistants, and rented a villa.

To begin the teaching, His Holiness gave the Chakrasamvara major initiation from the lineage of Krishnacarya and the blessing-initiation of the goddess herself. During the course of the guiding instructions, His Holiness also bestowed the body-mandala instruction, the uncommon meditation beyond thought, the ritual of 'showing the dharmata' and the initiation for Chitapati, the Protector Deities of this cycle. In addition, he gave the torma initiation of Khon Vajrakilaya, although it is not part of the Vajrayogini cycle of teaching.

Also present during this event was H.E. Jetsun Kushog, whom I had not seen since her visit to Bristol. She was prevailed upon to give the initiation of Red Tara. Finally, H.E. Gyana Vajra Rinpoche gave the initiations of White Manjushri Arapatsana from the Bari collection and the initiation of Bhutadamara.

Eight months later, the commitment that we had made back in 2005 to meet H.H. Karmapa was fulfilled when he returned to London in June 2007. This time, however, it turned out that there would not be the same degree of secrecy. Nevertheless, it began with a private meeting in South London, as before.

We took the opportunity to show a photograph of the beautiful house and gardens in Manchester which Kagyu Ling was attempting to purchase at that time. It was a former children's home on a quiet tree-lined road in the suburb of Chorlton, and had been administered by an order of Catholic nuns, making it a particularly auspicious acquisition for a dharma-centre. Unfortunately, the finances were tight. However, I asked His Holiness to bless the project, and, to everyone's astonishment and joy, three months later, the bank loans came through and Kagyu Ling had its new home.

On the day after our meeting, His Holiness was scheduled to give a White Tara initiation from the 9th Karmapa's collection known as 'Knowing One, Liberated in All' in central London for the Diamond Way. So, thinking that we could attend without it attracting attention, we confirmed to His Holiness that we would be there. However, all thoughts of secrecy had to be abandoned at the end of the initiation, when His Holiness made a general announcement expressing his pleasure at my presence. It was too late to keep it quiet!

I realised immediately that there were going to be some difficulties coming our way. The divisions among Kagyu followers made this certain, but I felt very happy and determined to go forward. It was like being reconnected to the half of the dharma-world from which we had so long been alienated. As a sign of that re-connection, His Holiness accepted my invitation to visit Kagyu Ling during his next European tour.

Rinpoche was soon with us again in London, and, during those days, he gave me the reading-transmission for three prayers composed by Tangtong Gyalpo and also for a special ritual entitled *The Flag of Victory* that he himself had composed for the Drala deities. This class of worldly deities, which includes King Gesar and Werma, are to be invoked for their assistance in accomplishing significant deeds. I would practice Rinpoche's ritual from time to time.

In my own teaching, I gave three Tara initiations: Green Tara from Atisha on my first visit to Sakya Dolma Ling in Mexico; Green Tara from the lineage of Shakyashribhadra in London; and the initiation and guiding instructions of White Tara the Wishfulfilling-Wheel in France. In addition, I gave the initiation of the obstacle-pacifying deity Achala, from the Bari Lotsava collection, in Bristol.

Some ten years earlier, Rinpoche had given me the celebrated text *The Union of Mahamudra and the Great Perfection* authored by Karma Chakme, which is a direct transmission that the latter had received from Chenrezi. It expressed much of the teachings on these twin contemplative streams that I had heard from Rinpoche and Ato Rinpoche, back in the 1970s. So, this year, I was pleased to give it both in Kagyu Ling and at Yeshe Nyingpo, during our second and soon to become annual trip to Los Angeles.

However, the major event of 2007 was undoubtedly the six-week visit of H.H. Sakya Trizin. The first week of His Holiness's stay in England was spent with us in Bristol. During this time, he gave the two-day major initiation of the three bodhisattvas (Manjushri, Chenrezi and Vajrapani), the 'lords of the three families' from the set of kriya tantras. As with the other major mandala initiations that I have received from His Holiness, this was drawn from *A Collection of Tantras*, compiled by Jamyang Khyentse Wangpo and Jamgon Loter Wangpo. It was followed by the series of initiations of the Twenty-One Taras from the lineage of Atisha. In private, His Holiness, gave me the reading-transmission for two short works by Sakya Pandita: *The Reply to Nyimo Gomchen* and *The Letter to the Holy Ones*.

The venue for the second and longer part of His Holiness's activity in England was the South Coast resort town of Bournemouth, where, some years earlier, a centre named Sakya Thubten Ling had been established. It was under the direction of Khenpo Jamyang Legshay, the director of Sakya Centre in Rajpur, and his brother, Khenpo Thubten Nyima. On this occasion, Khenpo Legshay had requested His Holiness to bestow the *Path and its Fruit* according to *The Explanation for The Assembly* (in Tibetan, *tshog shay*) and his relatively small sangha rose gallantly to the challenge of hosting this.

It was a precious opportunity to receive the *Path and its Fruit* for a second time. So, Albena and I, together with our son, Michael, who had just begun his legal training, rented a place in the town of Poole, close to the venue of the teachings. As His Holiness taught each day for five weeks, more or less without interruption, we were unable to venture far. I have to confess that, despite the town's proximity to the sea, it did not take long for Poole's charms to fade.

His Holiness commenced the cycle by bestowing the nine-deity initiation of Namgyalma from the lineage of Bari for the longevity of all participants. Then, utilising the texts composed by Ngawang Chodrak, he began by elucidating *The Three Visions*, interspersed with material on the history of the transmission lineage, also composed by Ngawang Chodrak. This preliminary section concluded with the Bodhisattva Vow according to the system of the *Path and its Fruit*.

At the beginning of the *Three Tantras*, His Holiness

bestowed the causal initiation of Hevajra, necessary for the exclusively tantric instructions to be bestowed upon those present. Having completed the first or *All-Base Causal Tantra*, which culminates with an exposition of the 'inseparability of samsara and nirvana', His Holiness then taught the outer development-stage practice of Hevajra, the very first part of the second or *Path Tantra*. In order for people to be able to receive the inner development-stage teaching, His Holiness bestowed the path initiation of Hevajra. For this part of the teaching, His Holiness gave detailed additional instruction from the two explanatory texts composed by Ngawang Chodrak that are to be used in conjunction with the elucidation of his own text on *The Three Tantras*.

At the conclusion of this part of the teaching, His Holiness bestowed the initiation of Virupa's Protection, subsequently going on to elucidate the completion-stage instructions derived from the three higher initiation paths. Then, at the end of the teaching of the third or *Mahamudra Fruition Tantra*, His Holiness bestowed the initiation of *The Profound Path of Guru-Yoga* and brought the entire cycle to a close.

Throughout this time, His Holiness taught each morning. In the afternoon, H.E. Ratna Rinpoche taught the material from the morning session again, and most days I led a group meditation session. About sixty people attended the whole teaching from many different countries. Some did not seem to know very much about dharma and were, understandably, bemused. Yet for others, it was a wonderful part of their Vajrayana education.

In February of the following year, we returned to Rajpur, where I had requested H.H. Sakya Trizin to bestow further extensive teachings. This time, His Holiness bestowed all the blessing-initiations for the eighty-four siddhas according to the lineage of the great sixteenth-century Jonang master, Jetsun Kunga Drolchog, which Rinpoche had begun to give some eight years previously in Nepal. On this occasion, His Holiness gave the initiations together with the reading-transmission of Abhayadatta's *History of the Eighty-Four Siddhas* and the collection of their Doha songs, accompanied by a commentary compiled by Vira Prakasha.

The stories and songs of these great Indian adepts of Vajrayana had been gathered originally by the eleventh-century master, Vajrasanapada. According to tradition, he had invited as many masters as he could to a ganapuja, at which each told the story of their realisation and offered a spontaneous doha song as an instruction. This had formed the basis for the subsequent composition of their history by Abhayadatta and the transmission of their initiations.

As was usual when I requested major teachings from His Holiness, in addition to offerings to the Vajra-master and important Tulkus, we made extensive tea offerings to those who attended, both the monastic sangha and some Tibetan lay-people.

On the way back from Rajpur, we took the opportunity to visit Karmapa International Buddhist Institute in Delhi to pay respects to H.H. Karmapa. I had never previously visited KIBI, as it was called. It was a joyful meeting with His Holiness, and, as luck would have it, Shamar Rinpoche was also there at that time. His Holiness insisted that we meet. So, more than twenty years since our last meeting, we had tea together. There was much to talk about.

In May, we flew to Los Angeles, where I taught Patrul Rinpoche's teaching *View, Meditation and Action* for

Yeshe Nyingpo Centre, and then flew down to Mexico City, where I gave various teachings and a public lecture for our centre, Sakya Dolma Ling. When you approached it from the air, Mexico City looked like a vast ocean made up of twenty million people, with dwellings seeming to reach beyond the horizon. Down below, I felt that I could hear Kerouac singing the *Mexico City Blues*. It is a city simultaneously beautiful and fearsome, where the dharma has to be genuine because real blood, suffering and passion have long flooded these streets.

Back in England, I gave various teachings that year: Atisha's *Jewel Rosary* and the initiations of Parnashabari and White Manjushri, both from Bari's collection, in Bristol, Chim Namkha Drak's *Mind-Training in a Single Session* in Exeter, the initiation of the Sixteen Arhats in Harrogate, the initiation of White Manjushri in London and Gampopa's *Precious Rosary of the Supreme Path* in Kagyu Ling.

Alongside these activities, I taught Tokme Zangpo's *Thirty-Seven Practices* in our centre in Stuttgart, after which we travelled on to Sofia. There, thanks to the efforts of my students Kaloyan and Petya Christov, the construction of our new house on the outskirts of Sofia had just been completed. Perched a little way up Lozen Mountain, it looks over the city spread out in the valley in front and the ancient Balkans rising in the middle distance. To our left, Vitosha, chief mountain of the city, stretches out like a sleeping guardian.

To render things auspicious for our new place and our dharma-activities there, I carried out the ritual of the Drala according to Rinpoche's text. As I threw the barley offerings, a powerful storm instantaneously arose from a clear blue sky. The sky itself went dark; a ferocious wind started to blow, accompanied by torrential rain. It threatened to destroy the small shrine that we had made for the ritual and scatter the pages of the prayers.

Nevertheless, I persisted, and, as soon as I concluded the Drala ritual, I recited the Serkyem offering ritual to our Sakya Protectors. With that, the storm and wind immediately subsided and the sky cleared. The local gods and spirits, it seemed, had wanted to meet the Drala and Protectors with an elaborate display of their own power, but had been calmed by Gonpo Gur and his entourage.

Perhaps the most significant teaching that year was *Discriminating the Three Vows* by Sakya Pandita; I gave it at Sakya Changlochen Ling in the Dordogne. It had been over twenty-nine years since Rinpoche had taught this same text in Bristol.

Just before that, we had been very pleased to host H.E. Jetsun Kushog Rinpoche in Sakya Dechen Ling in Stuttgart. She gave teachings on *Parting from the Four Attachments* and the initiation of Red Tara the Heroine from Atisha's Twenty-One Taras.

The last major event of that year was our attendance at the Fifth Supreme Buddhist Summit, held in the same majestic headquarters of Nembutsu-shu that I had visited on my first trip to Japan. On this occasion, Albena came with me, and we took with us Jonathan, Kunga and the musician Phil Hudson. It was an impressive event and gathering. In addition to the various 'supreme Buddhist leaders', such as the patriarchs of the monastic sangha of Thailand, Laos and so on, there were also a number of royal dignitaries, such as Princess Ashi Dechen Wangmo from Bhutan, a disciple of Shamar Rinpoche. The chief guest of honour was the late Prince Norodom Sihanouk of Cambodia, one of the great survivors of South East Asian politics and a devout lay Theravadin.

Our hosts managed the whole event and accompanying sight-seeing trips to Kyoto with unfailing efficiency, good humour and patience. It was difficult not to be moved by their sincerity about the dharma. The conference ended with an impassioned speech from the patriarch of Nembutsu-shu and, at that time, President of the Summit, the most venerable Dr Kyuse Enshinjoh. He lamented the decline and destruction that has overtaken the dharma and urged all present to work for the restoration of its glories.

There was much to think about in this. Indeed, it had been on my mind for many years, especially as the excitement at the coming of dharma to the West has given way to a more sober understanding of the size of the task. Nevertheless, it is a task that has been accomplished before, in many times and places, and it can be done again. I have some confidence that the generations to come will prove themselves equal to this, even though they will have to overcome obstacles that we cannot yet see. In this work, they will have the support of the dharma-protectors, to whom we must pray for the continued flourishing of the teaching in the coming decades and centuries.

Chapter Eight
Two Thrones

As I reflected during my time in Japan, it must be due to the Buddha's extraordinary wisdom and skill that his teachings flowered in so many different traditions. When it comes to our own relationship with the dharma, perhaps our affinities with particular schools have been established through karmic patterning. In any case, although the 'four unbroken practices of Sakya'[3] are at the heart of my own daily practice, I have always had confidence in both Sakya and Kagyu since first meeting Rinpoche and His Holiness. This two-fold legacy would be very much to the forefront in the next few years.

The first major event of 2009 was our journey to Rajpur, where H.H. Sakya Trizin had kindly agreed to my request to bestow the initiations of Manjuvajra-Guhyasamaja and Lokeshvaravajra-Guhyasamaja. As I had already obtained Akshobyavajra-Guhyasamaja from him some years earlier, I would, by this means, now have acquired all three chief forms of Guhyasamaja, the major father-line anuttara tantra. I was very happy about that, because, since Sachen Kunga Nyingpo received it from Lama Namkha'upa and Bari Lotsava in the twelfth century, Guhyasamaja has been considered one of the principal tantric cycles of our tradition.

After these two initiations, His Holiness bestowed Jamgon Loter Wangpo's guiding instructions on the development and completion stage practices of Manjuvajra. This particular Guhyasamaja completion-stage practice differs greatly from what is found in the Hevajra or Chakrasamvara cycles, both of which emphasise the techniques of chandali and mandala-chakra, whereas here it is the yoga of the illusory body that is the key completion-stage practice. Of course, Hevajra and Chakrasamvara have been most influential for me, but it was helpful to have some notion of the Guhyasamaja approach.

His Holiness also bestowed Jetsun Drakpa Gyaltsen's Commentary on Chandragomin's *Twenty Verses*. This famous work presents the discipline associated with the Bodhisattva Vow of the Mind-Only lineage.

Apart from this trip to India, I made two other intercontinental journeys that year, going to Los Angeles in the spring to give the initiations of Green Tara from Atisha's Lineage and Manjushri from Bari Lotsava at Yeshe Nyingpo, and in the autumn to Sakya Dolma Ling in Mexico to teach the White Tara guiding instructions and give the initiations of Chenrezi-Mahamudra and White Manjushri. In Los Angeles, I also taught Dampa Sangye's *One Hundred Pieces of Advice* and, in Mexico, Tokme Zangpo's commentary on *The Seven Points of Mind-Training*.

Back in England, in Bristol, I taught *The Seven Points of Mind-Training* as well but, on this occasion, I drew upon the commentary by Geshe Se Chilbupa, a direct disciple of Geshe Chekhawa. *The Seven Points* themselves are essentially a Mahayana system of practice for maintaining and strengthening bodhichitta, the very cause of entering the bodhisattva path. Thus its famed techniques such as 'sending and taking' (in Tibetan, *tonglen*) and the analytical and settling phases of meditating on ultimate bodhichitta were never intended to be abstracted from this setting and divested of their purpose.

Unfortunately, nowadays, these practices are often cannibalised by the therapy industry or even by followers of other religions. It seems that this has come about because the radically Mahayana nature of *Mind-Training* has been ignored in favour of selling it as 'self-help' or 'feel good' sentimentality. In such a way, the liberating force of the dharma is compromised and deteriorates, just as happens to medicines, when they are misused and prescribed inappropriately.

Incidentally, it seems to me that, if we are not vigilant, a similar fate may befall our Vajrayana teachings also. Indeed, in the U.S.A., one often sees members of non-Buddhist groups attending initiations in blithe ignorance or disregard of the fact that these depend upon the exclusive commitment to Buddhism that is entailed by Taking Refuge and making the Bodhisattva Vow, steps that always preface initiations. One fears that such cultists and spiritual entrepreneurs are simply shopping for exciting techniques to market to their customers. I hope that the men and women of the next dharma generation reaffirm the inviolability of our teachings and thus cast out this corruption.

For Kagyu Ling, I gave Patrul Rinpoche's *View, Meditation and Action*, the same text that I had taught in Los Angeles a year earlier and then, at the end of the year, I taught the first half of Situ Tenpai Nyingje's Commentary on *Rangjung Dorje's Aspiration Prayer of Mahamudra*. I would teach the second half the following Christmas. It had been thirty years since Rinpoche had taught this text, a work that is famous not only for the profundity of its teaching but also for its literary qualities, appropriately enough for something composed by as celebrated a linguist and grammarian as the 8th Situ.

I visited Stuttgart three times during that year of 2009, giving Chenrezi-Mahamudra and White Manjushri. The third visit was actually to welcome Gyana Vajra Rinpoche, the younger of H.H. Sakya Trizin's two sons, who was visiting us on his first solo dharma tour of the West. He bestowed the initiation of Sangye Menla from the lineage of Shantarakshita, and spent a free day in a specially conducted tour of the Daimler factory, where Wolfgang was employed as a senior scientist.

Two years earlier, H.H. Karmapa had accepted my invitation to visit Kagyu Ling, and he had re-confirmed this when we met in Delhi a year later. Now, in July 2009, the visit was to happen. His Holiness had actually begun his European tour a month earlier at Karma Gön, a centre just outside of Malaga, which had been established by Pedro and Dorrit Gomez. This warmhearted and resourceful Spanish-Danish couple, who were disciples of Lama Ole Nydahl, had rendered a lot of assistance to H.H. Karmapa and his family.

Albena and I flew to Southern Spain to see him at Karma Gön. His Holiness's father, Mipham Rinpoche, and Ma Yum-la, his mother, were staying there at the time, and so we enjoyed a family meal all together, presided over by His Holiness. Despite his stroke and confinement in a wheelchair, Mipham Rinpoche had a presence and sharpness of mind about him. It's easy to see what a great support both His Holiness's parents have been for him.

A month later, His Holiness arrived in England. We had arranged a meeting with the Lord Mayor of Manchester. It took place in the city's impressive Gothic

Revival town hall, conveniently close to the venue that we had hired for the scheduled four days of teaching. For the general public, as well as our community, His Holiness taught Tokme Zangpo's *Thirty-Seven Practices*. Around four hundred people attended. This was followed by the initiation of White Tara from the 9th Karmapa's collection. Finally, he bestowed the initiation of the 2nd Karmapa, Karma Pakshi, just as his predecessor had done on his visit to Manchester, almost thirty-two years earlier.

At the celebratory gathering we held for His Holiness at the end of this five days, I was able to introduce some of those, like the old-timer Jim Mullany, who had been present during that previous visit.

Before His Holiness left the country, we received the initiation of Marpa from him in London. Then, in Dhagpo Kagyu Ling, we obtained the initiation of Choling's Vajrasattva. It felt somewhat special to spend time with His Holiness in Dhagpo, his seat in Europe, established in the lifetime of his predecessor. Now, under the direction of the much-loved Jigme Rinpoche, and his hard-working administrative team headed by the President of the Dhagpo Association, Lama Jean-Guy, it was, in a sense, the headquarters for all Karma-Kagyu groups in Europe. It occurred to me that our Kagyu centres, for so long on the periphery, had now come in from the cold.

A month or so later, some of our efforts in the U.S.A. came to fruition, when we were able to purchase a small property in Santa Monica to serve as a new centre: Sakya Samten Ling. Fred Tyler from London, who is, happily enough, half-American, had led the negotiations for this, and would then continue to serve on the administrative team. Some years later, we would be able to relocate the centre to a spot just off fashionable Main Street, close to the border with Venice Beach, and therefore ideally located for the light drizzle of demi-celebrities who would attend our classes for a few weeks between yoga, mindfulness and A.A. meetings. Some regular people have come too, and some of them have stayed with the dharma.

Early in the following year of 2010, Gyana Vajra Rinpoche followed up his visit to our centre in Stuttgart with teachings in Bristol and London, giving the initiations of Sangye Menla, Manjushri Arapatsana and an initiation for the *Seven Line Prayer to Padmasambhava* from the lineage of Dudjom Rinpoche.

In England that same year at Kagyu Ling, I taught Drakpa Gyaltsen's commentary on *The King of Aspiration Prayers*, which I had received thirty-two years earlier from Rinpoche, and also bestowed the initiations of the One Thousand-Armed Chenrezi and Amitabha. In Harrogate, I gave the initiations of Manjushri Lion Speech from *A Collection of Sadhanas* and Choling Vajrasattva.

In Bristol, I gave the transmission for Amitabha 'transference' composed by Jamyang Kunga Tenpai Gyaltsen and the initiation of Simhamukha from the *Thirteen Golden Dharmas*, while in London I gave the initiation of Black Manjushri, also from the *Thirteen Golden Dharmas*. I visited both Germany and Bulgaria a number of times that year, giving teachings on *Mind-Training*, *Parting from the Four Attachments* and *The Fifty Verses on the Lama* and also the initiations of Gonkar, Sakya Pandita, Green Tara, White Saraswati and Amitayus, this last being from the Taklung Kagyu lineage.

However, the major event of the year was the visit made by H.H. Sakya Trizin in June. On this occasion, we hosted His Holiness in our apartment in London. For the general public, His Holiness taught *Parting from the Four Attachments* at the historic Inns of Court. Subsequently, he bestowed the major initiation of Kalachakra from the Vajramala Collection of Abhayakaragupta, the mediaeval Indian master. Five hundred people, including some Nyingma, Gelug and Kagyu followers, attended this two-day event in Kensington Town Hall.

Although the Kalachakra cycle does not occupy a central place in our spiritual syllabus, due to the prominence of Hevajra and Vajrayogini, nonetheless there have been some Sakya masters who have cultivated it, such as Chogye Tri Rinpoche. According to tradition, this non-dual anuttara tantra system was originally transmitted by Shakyamuni to King Suchandra in southern India and was then preserved in the kingdom of Shambhala for over a thousand years, before being brought back to India by Chelupa. Nowadays, some masters say that merely by receiving the initiation, one will be reborn in Shambhala in the lifetime of the 25th Kalki monarch, Rudra Chakrin, and thus be able to assist him in his defence of the dharma.

His Holiness also took the time to visit Sakya Thubten Ling in Bournemouth, where he bestowed the causal initiation of Hevajra. Apart from the blessing of receiving Hevajra again from His Holiness, it was also an opportunity to renew our acquaintance with the English sea-side. On this occasion, we eschewed Poole for the more genteel charms of Bournemouth itself.

There were some significant new developments that year. To begin with, Jigme Rinpoche and the administration team at Dhagpo Kagyu Ling asked me to give a short teaching on Madhyamaka philosophy there. It was simple enough to make the thirty-minute journey across the Vézère Valley from Changlochen, where I had been in retreat after giving Vajrapani Bhutadamara initiation and guiding instructions.

Secondly, our daughter Rosalind, together with Paul and our grandson Dominic, moved to New York. We stayed with them in their apartment in mid-town Manhattan over Christmas. During those days, we met up with James Shaheen, editor of Tricycle, the largest Buddhist magazine in the U.S.A., together with some of his staff. It was a meeting that had been arranged by Pamela Gayle White, a talented translator and teacher from Bodhi Path, who had been working with the publication for some time. As a result, I would contribute to the Tricycle on-line magazine a number of articles concerning the reception of dharma in the West.

Manhattan was cold that Christmas time, just as it had been four years earlier in San Francisco, but, walking around the Village, I wondered whether you could be nostalgic for a place that previously you had only visited in books and music. We took a few photos on Jones Street, just off West Fourth, and some more on McDougal Street, standing outside Caffe Dante, looking at the town-houses opposite.

Being in New York also gave us the chance to visit Tsechen Kunchab Ling, H.H. Sakya Trizin's new seat in North America. It was located in the small town of Walden, about ninety minutes by car from Manhattan. There we met Khenpo Kelsang, who had steered the centre from its inception. Just after leaving New York to return to London, I accomplished a retreat on Hevajra, and then travelled to Stuttgart to give Jetsun Drakpa's Red Tara Initiation, my first teaching of 2011.

April was spent in California where, at Sakya Samten Ling, I taught Gorampa's *Parting from the Four Attachments* and gave the initiations of Shakyashri's Green

Tara and the goddess Simhamukha from the *Thirteen Golden Dharmas*. At Yeshe Nyingpo, I again gave the magnetizing Red Tara initiation. During our time there, we stayed in a Malibu beach-house; a dwelling that was kindly loaned to us on a quite a few occasions in those years. It was a beautiful place. In the day-time, you could watch the dolphins dance and, a little further out, the whales shadowing the coast-line. In the night-time, the moon would carve a path in reflected light through the ocean. Who knows where that path ends? You could see some interesting things at the Malibu Country Mart, too, as well as up on Point Dume.

It is not that I neglected England in 2011. In Kagyu Ling, I taught the 9th Karmapa's *Mahamudra Clearing the Clouds of Unawareness*; at Kagyu Dechen Dzong, in Harrogate, I gave the initiation of Amitayus from the Taklung tradition. As for Sakya teachings, I gave Green Tara and Simhamukha initiations in Bristol, and, in London, I gave the weath-deity, Black Dzambhala, from Bari Lotsava, and the initiation of Manjushri in connection with the 'Gangloma' prayer.

At the time of this last initiation in November, Karma Thinley Rinpoche was staying with us on his way back to Toronto from Kathmandu, a journey he has made every year for over thirty years. His presence in London created the opportunity for the one hundred people, attending the day of teaching, to receive the reading-transmission for his *Telescope of Wisdom* directly from him. It was the first time that Rinpoche had given any public teaching in England since the Vajravarahi initiation, some nine years earlier in Manchester.

In May, earlier that year, Albena and I had spent some time at the Phodrang in Rajpur. I had requested His Holiness for the major initiation of Chakrasamvara from the lineage of the siddha Vajraghanta. The Sakya tradition preserves three principal lines of Chakrasamvara, which were originally transmitted in India through the three siddhas: Krishnacharya, Luipa and Vajraghanta. I had received the first two of these previously, and so now I was able to obtain the initiation for the third and final line.

According to tradition, the Chakrasamvara cycle, having first been proclaimed in the pure realms like all tantras, later spread in the human world. Unlike other tantras, however, its mandala is still to be found here, as it consists of twenty-four sacred places located throughout India, where the Buddha in the form of Heruka subdued the wordly gods that embody the energies of desire and hatred. Since Vajrayogini herself is the consort of Chakrasamvara, this tantra is a crucial source for her meditation. Hence, I felt that it was very important to have this support for my practice.

Over the four days following Chakrasamvara, His Holiness also gave the initiations for the Twenty-One Taras according to the Indian master, Suryagupta. Each of the twenty-one forms of the goddess is associated with one of the four 'activities' – pacifying, increasing, magnetising or wrathful.

Subsequently, His Holiness bestowed the initiations for the Four Kadam Deities. In fact, Karma Thinley Rinpoche had bestowed this last set of initiations many years previously, but, at that time, it had been in accordance with the system contained in the *Treasury of Spiritual Instructions*. Now, on this occasion, His Holiness gave them according to the lineage preserved in *A Collection of Sadhanas*.

Passing through Delhi on our way back to Europe, we stopped in at KIBI to have lunch with H.H. Karmapa. After that, we were in quite a hurry to get back, as H.E.

Ratna Vajra Rinpoche was due to arrive in Stuttgart a few days later. There, in Germany, Ratna Rinpoche gave teachings on Gorampa Sonam Sengge's *Discriminating the Madhyamaka View* and the initiation of Amitabha from *A Collection of Sadhanas*.

Three months later, Ratna Rinpoche would join us in Bristol to continue these Madhyamaka teachings, and give the major initiation of Vajrakilaya according to the Khon lineage. At the end of that initiation, Ratna Rinpoche asked me to teach Sapan's brief text on the *Fourteen Root Downfalls* to guide those present in the maintenance of the Vajrayana vows and pledges that they had just made in the course of the initiation. For Sakya Dechen Ling in London, Ratna Rinpoche gave Manjushri Arapatsana initiation and also took the time to bless our centre and give the reading-transmission for the *Manjushri Namasamgiti*.

Between Ratna Rinpoche's teachings in Germany and England, the historic visit of his father, H.H. Sakya Trizin, to Sakya Dolma Ling in Mexico took place. He was accompanied by Gyal Yum Chenmo-la and Gyana Vajra Rinpoche. Most of our family was there too, Rosalind having just received *The Path and its Fruit* from His Holiness in Walden. It gave the visit the feeling of a warm and lovely family occasion, despite the rain-filled July weather. To several hundred people, His Holiness taught *Parting From The Four Attachments*, and gave the initiation of Manjushri and the torma initiation of Vajrakilaya.

2012 began for me with a White Tara retreat, undertaken on the advice of H.H. Karmapa. According to astrology a 'difficult year' was coming for all those born in 'dragon' years, as both Albena and I had been, albeit with a twelve-year gap between us. It had been some time since

I had last done Tara retreat but, after a few days, you always discover that the deity has been naturally present all the time. You just need to be spacious enough to let her manifest. It's the same with all our yidam practice, both inside and outside of retreat situations.

Rinpoche's commentary on *The Letter to a Friend* was a major feature of my teaching throughout the year, in both Manchester and Stuttgart. Nagarjuna's root-text is very suitable for people new to Buddhism, as it gives such a clear presentation of the three trainings – moral discipline, meditation and wisdom – common to all traditions of dharma. Alongside this, I gave the initiations of Black Manjushri, White Manjushri, Yellow Dzambhala, Choling's Vajrasattva and Vajrakilaya, Namgyalma, Prajnaparamita and Vasudhara from Bari's Collection and Lion Speech Manjushri in our centres in England. In Bristol, I also taught Tsarchen's commentary on *The Fifty Verses on The Lama*, alongside the initiations I gave there.

In spring, we visited Los Angeles and Mexico City. In the first of these, I gave the initiations of Chenrezi-Mahamudra and White Saraswati in our own centre, and, for Yeshe Nyingpo, I gave a teaching on the *Four Seals*. I gave Saraswati, once more, at our centre in Mexico, together with Shantarakshita's Menla initiation and teachings on *Mind-Training*.

We were back in the U.S.A. in early June to attend the Rime Monlam in up-state New York. This event was the idea of two American dharma-teachers: Tulku Sherdor and Lama Surya Das. Tulku Sherdor had a background as a translator and practitioner in the Kagyu and Nyingma traditions, his principal master being the late Kusum Lingpa from Eastern Tibet. Lama Surya was the better known of the two, with many published books to his name and a long friendship with the late Baba Ramdass, the American spiritual celebrity. My invitation came via Moke Mokotoff, the Oriental Art specialist and long-time Sakyapa.

This Monlam was inspired by the success of the annual Monlam festivals that have been held by the four great traditions in Bodhgaya over the last two decades. The central focus of these gatherings is the collective recitation of aspiration prayers, such as the bodhisattva Samantabhadra's *Prayer of Excellent Conduct* for the benefit of all sentient beings. Unlike the Monlams held in India, this new event was designed to include all Vajrayana schools. It took place over three days in the Garrison Institute, close to West Point but on the other side of the Hudson River.

Shortly after this, we flew to India, where in Rajpur, H.H. Sakya Trizin bestowed the major initiation of Sangye Menla from the kriya tantras and the Five-Deity Manjushri from the charya tantras. Both initiations were drawn from *The Collection of Tantras*. Just as importantly, at my request, His Holiness gave the reading-transmission for *The Treasury of Esoteric Instructions*. This so-called 'Black Volume' of the *Path and its Fruit*, is an extraordinary commentary on Virupa's root verses, composed by the 15th Sakya Trizin, Lama Dampa Sonam Gyaltsen, in the fourteenth century. This two-day transmission was very restricted, and, consequently, took place in His Holiness's shrine-room in the Phodrang itself.

Since that time, Lama Dampa's remarkable text has exerted a major influence on my understanding and practice of *The Path and its Fruit*. It is the most detailed of the various expositions of the root-verses and contains many elements which are not found in the eleven commentaries that Sachen Kunga Nyingpo bestowed directly upon his disciples. Auspiciously enough, the previous year, we had sponsored a statue of Lama Dampa for the new temple at Tsechen Kunchab Ling.

In early July, H.H. Karmapa arrived in Manchester for his second visit. During this time, he bestowed the major initiation of Gyalwa Gyamtso, an anuttara form of Red Chenrezi, and one of the three key yidam practices of the Karma-Kagyu, alongside Vajravarahi and Chakrasamvara. He also managed to visit Kagyu Dechen Dzong in Harrogate, where he gave the Milarepa initiation, just as his predecessor had done in Manchester thirty-five years earlier. Subsequently, for the Diamond Way in London, he gave the initiation of White Dzambhala from the lineage of Atisha. We then travelled on to Dhagpo in France, where His Holiness gave several days of teachings on Shantideva's *Entering the Path of a Bodhisattva* and the Chenrezi initiation from *Knowing One, Liberated in All*.

Immediately His Holiness left Dhagpo, we moved across the valley to Sakya Changlochen Ling, where I began to teach Sakya Pandita's Mahayana graduated path treatise, *Elucidating the Thought of the Sage*, which would take me three visits to complete.

The second week was dedicated to White Tara retreat. As soon as this was finished, I returned to Dhagpo, where I gave a two-day teaching on Madhyamaka, before journeying on to Kundreul Ling in the Auvergne. There, His Holiness Karmapa gave the initiation of Mahakala Dorje Bernagchen.

It had already been an extraordinarily hectic summer but there were three more trips before the year's end.

In late October, we visited Los Angeles for the second time that year. At the request of the Yeshe Nyingpo sangha, I taught the *Four Dharmas of Gampopa*, while, for

Sakya Samten Ling, I gave the initiation of the wealth-deity, Vasudhara, from the *Collection of Bari Lotsava*.

The next month saw us return to India, where, at H.H. Karmapa's suggestion, I had been invited to give five days of teaching on *The Four Dharmas*. Subsequently, I would be appointed as one of KIBI's visiting faculty, alongside Beru Khyentse Rinpoche, Khenpo Chodrak Tenphel and Dupseng Rinpoche.

KIBI is situated in the Mehrauli district of South Delhi. It's in a spot given over to institutions and hospitals, and faces directly on to a large park, which is inviting by day and forbidding by night. The land itself was actually given to H.H. the 16th Karmapa by the Indian Government in 1979 but the building and the Institute itself had to be brought to completion by Shamar Rinpoche. KIBI finally opened in 1990, and is nowadays part-monastery and part-educational institute, providing courses on dharma to visiting students from across the West and from the Chinese diaspora. H.H. Karmapa and Shamar Rinpoche installed the scholar Professor Sempa Dorje as the academic head of the Institute. He was a close disciple of the famed Kunu Rinpoche, hailing from the same Indo-Tibetan ethnic group, and had previously worked at the prestigious Sanskrit University of Varanasi.

After this teaching at KIBI was completed, we travelled up again to Rajpur to see H.H. Sakya Trizin. His Holiness gave the transmission for the commentary on Virupa's root verses of the *Path and its Fruit* taught by Sachen Kunga Nyingpo to his disciple, Geshe Nyag. This particular text is quite a lot shorter than the commentary by Lama Dampa that he had given to us in May, but it is the most commonly used guide to the root verses. I had also asked His Holiness for the transmission of the Tibetan siddha Tsembupa's guiding instructions on

Chenrezi practice. On this occasion, the great meditator Chiwang Tulku also came to receive the transmission with us. He had done the same for the *Thirteen Golden Dharmas*, back in 1986.

The way that His Holiness taught during these days was, as always, with a patient, detailed unfolding of the intelligence of the dharma. It is as if one is receiving the teaching directly from Manjushri himself. At the same time, His Holiness maintains complete fidelity to the precision of the teaching. Due to this, his disciples come to possess the necessary understanding and confidence to enter into the practice themselves, sure that everything they need has been given to them, like apprentices thoroughly schooled by a master-craftsman endowed with unfailing kindness and compassion.

By mid-2013, my teachings on *The Telescope of Wisdom* at Kagyu Ling came to an end, to be followed by another of Rinpoche's commentaries – *The Lamp Dispelling Darkness* – his exposition of Karmapa Rangjung Dorje's *Discriminating between Consciousness and Primordial Wisdom*. Ganesha Press had, in fact, just brought out a new translation of this produced by Adrian O'Sullivan.

In general terms, Rangjung Dorje's text and its companion, *Showing the Buddha-Nature*, are viewed as works presenting Zhentong Madhyamaka, or, as it is sometimes styled, The Great Madhyamaka. However, *Discriminating between Consciousness and Primordial Wisdom* contains an in-depth analysis of the workings of the eight types of consciounesses, as they are delineated in the Chittamatra school of tenets, and this utilisation of such material reveals why this Zhentong approach may also be termed Yogachara Madhyamaka. In the course of this work, Rangjung Dorje explains how these samsaric aspects of mind are transmuted into the primordial wisdom, which has, in a sense, always been their real nature. As Rinpoche brings out in his commentary, according to the Zhentong perspective, such a transformation is possible precisely because samsara and nirvana rest on the buddha-nature as their basis.

In Kagyu Ling's sister-centre, Kagyu Dechen Dzong, I taught Dampa Sangye's *One Hundred Pieces of Advice*, while, in Bristol and London, I gave Jetsun Drakpa Gyaltsen's commentary on *The Twenty Verses* and Tokme Zangpo's commentary on *The Seven Points of Mind-Training* respectively.

That summer in Dhagpo Kagyu Ling, I taught Jamgon Kongtrul's *Rays of the Vajra Moon*, his elucidation of how one should meditate on the Zhentong Madhyamaka view. I would actually end up teaching this text, which I had received from Rinpoche back in the '80s, in many places over the years to come.

Our first trip to California that year had begun near the end of March, when we flew to Los Angeles. There, I gave the initiation of Sangye Menla and taught Tokme Zangpo's *The Thirty-Seven Practices*. We then travelled up through the vast, featureless Central Valley to San Francisco and Berkeley, where Ewam Choden was located.

This centre and its head lama, Thartse Shabdrung Rinpoche (known as Lama Kunga), had invited me to teach on Madhyamaka for a couple of days. I was very happy to accede to this, because he was the younger brother of Thartse Khen Rinpoche, who had been so helpful to me at the beginning of the 1980s. From the centre's shrine-room, you can look out across the Bay to Marin County and Alcatraz island. When it's foggy there, the outlook is transformed and you feel like you are sailing on a sea of mist. It's certainly a great spot for a dharma-centre, and Lama Kunga's warmth and erudition have inspired a small but dedicated group of students, who have stayed with him through the years.

From San Francisco, we flew down to Mexico, where I gave the initiations of Yellow Dzambhala and Green Tara. The weekend was given over to the Bhutadamara initiation and guiding instructions, the most detailed Vajrayana teaching that I had explained there. It is usually seen as a practice that protects one from the obstacles, internal or external, that might arise in our practice of the major anuttara cycles, such as Hevajra and Vajrayogini.

From there it was back to London, where, at the beginning of May, Karma Thinley Rinpoche flew in, on the way to Nepal. A couple of years earlier, Rinpoche had composed a small text, *The Telescope of Faith*, as an explanation of the distinction between definitive and provisional dharma and the relationship between dharma and science. Now, on this occasion, Rinpoche gave me the reading-transmission for this important work.

A couple of weeks after this, we flew to New York, a visit that had been arranged the previous autumn, when we had been with H.H. Sakya Trizin in Rajpur. At that time, I had requested various Dharma Protector initiations, which permit one to practise their individual rituals, but His Holiness had suggested that it would be more appropriate to give them privately, when he was in residence in the Phodrang in Walden. So, in late May, joined by Rosalind and our grandson, Dominic, we rented a house in the town of New Paltz, in up-state New York, for a week. It was convenient for daily travel to Walden but also close enough to Woodstock to pay a fleeting visit to that historic town, with its arts and crafts ambience.

We had seen something of the Hudson River Valley, travelling up to the Rime Monlam in the Garrison Institute from Manhattan, the previous year. For much of the way, the train travels beside the river, passing through stations with Native American names like Manitou, reminding you how recently the U.S.A. has been set down on this ancient land. The Hudson's quiet grandeur was really unexpected; I could understand why this area has attracted so many painters and other artists for the last century or so, not to mention the numerous dharma-centres, that have grown here more recently.

The post-industrial town of Walden itself, where Tsechen Kunchab Ling is located, sits on the seemingly less favoured south side of the Hudson River. By contrast with the rather affluent area around the Garrison Institute, it seems not to be faring so well. In such a place, Tsechen Kunchab Ling, with its newly-constructed traditional temple, is well-positioned to radiate the uplifting spirit of dignity and kindness that is intrinsic to the dharma.

Over several days His Holiness bestowed the initiations of the Three Deities of Panjaranatha (in Tibetan, *Gonpo Gur Lha Sum*) the Eight Deities of Panjaranatha (in Tibetan, *Gonpo Gur Lha Gyay*), Tathagatarakshita's Four-Faced Mahakala, Mahakali Parvati Rajni and Begtse, all from *A Collection of Sadhanas*. A very powerful atmosphere reigned in the temple during these days of the initiations of these deities, all of whose rituals bestow a two-fold protection – guarding the practitioners themselves from obstacles, internal and external, and preventing the dissipation of spiritual accomplishment. Apart from ourselves, there were only Khenpo Pema and Khenpo Kelsang, together with his assistant, Ani Kunga, present.

Back in Europe, Albena and I had been invited to the inauguration of Dhagpo Kagyu Ling's impressive new Institute, which was due to take place in June, with H.H. Karmapa presiding. However, at the last moment, owing to the indisposition of his father, His Holiness was forced to cancel. So, as second head of the Karma-Kagyu tradition, Shamar Rinpoche stepped into the breach.

Fortunately for everybody present, in addition to conducting the actual ceremony of consecrating the Institute, Rinpoche bestowed two days of teaching on Rangjung Dorje's *Aspiration Prayer of Mahamudra,* and gave the two-day major initiation of Gyalwa Gyamtso.

On the last night, we had an enjoyable private dinner with Rinpoche. Many stories of mutual acquaintances were recounted, and Rinpoche explained his reasons for setting up the Bodhi Path organisation in North America and Europe. He revealed that it had been motivated particularly by a concern to counter distorted presentations of Kagyu dharma which had emerged in the West; it was very helpful to get Rinpoche's perspective. Finally, that evening, we made plans for Rinpoche's visit to Kagyu Ling to take place in the summer of 2014 – a prospect that filled me with happiness.

That year of 2013 had another significance; it was the twenty-fifth anniversary of the founding of Tegchen Legshay Ling, and Karma Thinley Rinpoche had expressly invited us to be present for this celebration. So we flew to Nepal for five days. While we were there, the nunnery's ordained sangha performed long-life rituals for Rinpoche and myself.

Being in Bodhnath caused me to reflect on monasticism and its future a little. Although our own dharma-community in the West is entirely lay, and both the Sakya and Kagyu traditions were established in Tibet by married tantric masters, Sachen Kunga Nyingpo and Marpa Lotsava respectively, I cannot imagine a dharma utterly devoid of monasticism; it would be a dharma that had been stripped of one of its chief pillars. As it says in *The Sutra of Recollecting the Three Jewels*:

The sangha are the glorious field of merit[4]

In this lies the significance of our support for Rinpoche's nuns at Legshay Ling and those of the Sakya nunnery in Dehra Dun, as well as of our friendship with Dhagpo Kundreul Ling, a Western monastic institution that has survived for over three decades. Yet, for monasticism to endure in the West, and in Asia, there may need to be a recalibration of the numbers of monastics, to endow it with an enduring economic base, and a re-thinking of the age at which people enter the monastic life. In fact, Rinpoche himself remarked on these points to me many years ago.

Since it had been ten years since our last visit to Kathmandu, we took the opportunity to revisit nearby Pharping, where Rinpoche had recently constructed a small retreat-centre. We made offerings at the Vajrayogini temple and prayers at the upper cave of Guru Padmasambhava. In comparison to Kathmandu itself, which had become extremely dense with new developments – new monasteries, new houses, new people – Pharping felt more or less the same as twenty-five years earlier. There was still space between the monasteries and retreat-centres and even the holy spots there had a stillness that I had feared would have been lost by now.

Back in England, in September, I gave a presentation on 'Padmasambhava and Sakya' at a conference on Pad-masambhava, arranged by the Zhang Zhung Institute of Namkhai Norbu Rinpoche. It was a day that mixed dharma and academia in a positive fashion. The venue was the School of Oriental and African Studies, and the day included old friends and now distinguished scholars like Geoffrey Samuel and Rob Meyer. I had discussed my paper a few months earlier with His Holiness, while we were in the US, and, consequently, I had something to contribute.[5]

Just after this came an invitation to attend a one-day conference of dharma teachers. It was to be hosted by the Insight Centre in mid-town Manhattan, and some of the big names in American Buddhism would attend. Since the invitation was relayed by Tulku Sherdor and Lama Surya Das, I felt that I had to accept it. I wasn't entirely convinced that it was my cup of tea, but it provided, at least, an opportunity to spend a few days in the Village. As for the conference itself, everybody was polite enough, but, during the whole day, I had the sensation of being a stranger in a strange land, where somehow the language sounds vaguely familiar but you can't quite make sense of it.

Naturally, there were exceptions, like Tulku Sherdor, but it seemed that most people there were on a quest to make the dharma 'relevant'. However, I think that such efforts only render it quickly dated. The reality to which dharma points is timeless. The young people who will make the dharma their own in the future will be the ones who know that. They won't want a watered-down, 'secular' or 'modern' Buddhism; they will want the power that will transform their lives.

At the moment, many Buddhist circles in the West are run by like-minded people in networks of recipro-cal patronage, all promoting a seemingly modern, po-litically and culturally monochrome version of dharma. In reality, this is as dead on arrival as the 'death of God' Christianity craze of the 1960s. Only the truly radical and counter-cultural will survive, because that is the only form of dharma that has power.

For me, it's the tradition passed from person to person

that transmits that power. It's like the stories in the ancient songs – Matty Groves and Black Jack Davy, who come riding up one day, whistling loud and merry, or the mysterious stranger from The House Carpenter surfacing from hell, after five hundred years, as the Man in the Long Black Coat, and all of them still wanting to charm the heart of a lady and carry her off to Italy. The truth of such songs can't be invented by some committee. It's the truth of many generations, and it's still the truth today. It's the truth that crossed the Atlantic from Northern England to be sung in the Appalachians. It's the truth of Virgil descending into the house of death with Aeneas, and, twelve hundred years later, guiding Dante along that narrow passageway in the bardo of Purgatory. Who could fabricate these things, and who ever talked about anything more important than them?

No one person made this stuff up. It can bust your brains out, just like Athena did to Zeus. It passed through each poet and each singer – they gave something to it, but none of them own it. The dharma's the same. That's why I knew that I had to find the living tradition – it wasn't in books and it wasn't in societies, because all that just added up to one big lie, and it definitely is not to be found in a 'reformation' of Buddhism.

Of course, there have been those looking for hidden traditions in the West – Eliphas Levi and Julius Evola, and all those types of people in France and Italy or the Golden Dawn people – Yeats, Mathers and Crowley – in London. However, they couldn't find anything but fragments of something that had been alive at one time, but was now long dead, and they mixed it up with fantasy and called it a tradition.

I read all that kind of thing once, but I could see that it was all too much of nothing. If a tradition doesn't lead us to the truth of reality, it's no use. Such a thing is no more than a pile of worthless fake antiques.

With such thoughts in my mind, we flew to Vienna, the Imperial Hapsburg capital, where the Karma-Kagyu Sangha, a group affiliated to Shamar Rinpoche's Bodhi Path network, had invited me to teach on the *Four Seals*. The group, led by the scholar Martina Dracszczyk and her psychotherapist husband, Alex, is the oldest Kagyu group in Austria, and occupies a space very close to the historic centre of the city. I lost count of how many dharma-groups they told us existed in Vienna. There are four Karma-Kagyu groups alone.

2013 then ended for us in California. Rosalind and Paul had relocated there; it meant that they would be nearer to our centre in Santa Monica. A few days before Christmas, Thartse Shabdrung Rinpoche came down for a couple of days from Berkeley, and gave the Menla initiation at Sakya Samten Ling.

Karma Thinley Rinpoche, India, 1970

Karma Thinley Rinpoche, Samye Ling, 1973

Kalu Rinpoche, Manchester, 1974

With Karma Thinley Rinpoche, Manchester, 1977

His Holiness 16th Karmapa and Jamgon Kongtrul
Rinpoche, 1977

Ato Rinpoche, Cambridge, 1978

With (*left to right*): His Holiness Sakya Gongma Trichen; His Holiness 42nd Sakya Trizin, Ratna Rinpoche; and Gyalyum Khenmo-la, Bristol, 1978

With Karma Thinley Rinpoche, Bristol, 1979

Ngor Phende Shabdrung Rinpoche, Bristol, 1979

Thartse Khen Rinpoche, Bristol, 1981

With His Holiness Sakya Gongma Trichen, Bristol, 1984

Bokar Rinpoche, Manchester, 1985

With Karma Thinley Rinpoche, Bodhnath, Nepal, 1988

With Karma Thinley Rinpoche, Liverpool, 1995

Bristol, 1998

With His Holiness Sakya Gongma Trichen, Bristol, 1998

Karma Thinley Rinpoche, Manchester, 2002

With Karma Thinley Rinpoche, Manchester, 2002

With His Holiness Sakya Gongma Trichen,
Sakya Centre, Rajpur, 2005

With His Holiness the 17th Karmapa,
KIBI, New Delhi, 2008

With His Holiness Sakya Gongma Trichen, Albena and
Katharina in the Phodrang, Rajpur, 2005

With His Holiness Sakya Gongma Trichen in the Phodrang, Rajpur, 2005.
Left to right: Her Eminence Dagmo Kalden; Her Eminence Gyalyum
Chenmo; His Holiness 42nd Sakya Trizin, Ratna Rinpoche; His Holiness
Sakya Gongma Trichen; Lama Jampa Thaye; Albena and Katharina.

With Shamar Rinpoche, KIBI, New Delhi, 2008

Her Eminence Jetsun Kushog Rinpoche, Stuttgart, 2008

With Albena, Japan, 2008

With His Holiness 17th Karmapa, Manchester, 2009

His Holiness 17th Karmapa, Manchester, 2009

With His Holiness Sakya Gongma Trichen, London, 2010

His Holiness Sakya Gongma Trichen, London, 2010

With His Eminence Gyana Vajra Rinpoche, London, 2010

With His Holiness 17th Karmapa, Manchester, 2012.
Left to right: Paul and Rosalind Haddon; Lama Jampa Thaye; His Holiness 17th Karmapa; Albena; Katharina; Dominic.

His Holiness 17th Karmapa, Manchester, 2012

Shamar Rinpoche, Manchester, 2014

With Shamar Rinpoche, Manchester, 2014

At Sakya Changlochen Ling, France, 2015

With (*left to right*) His Holiness 17th Karmapa, Acharya
Sempa Dorje, Khenpo Tsering, KIBI, 2015

With Karma Thinley Rinpoche, London, 2015

At Bodhgaya, 2017

With His Holiness Sakya Gongma Trichen,
Los Angeles, 2018

His Holiness Sakya Gongma Trichen, Los Angeles, 2018

His Holiness Sakya Gongma Trichen, Los Angeles, 2018

His Holiness 42nd Sakya Trizin, Ratna Rinpoche,
Mexico, 2018

His Holiness 42nd Sakya Trizin, Ratna Rinpoche,
Mexico, 2018

With His Holiness 42nd Sakya Trizin, Ratna Rinpoche and
Albena, Mexico, 2018

With Albena, Montchardon, 2019

Montchardon, 2019

Chapter Nine
Wandering in the World

Musing on the dharma world that Christmas in California, things looked like they might get to be interesting, but the only thing that you can know for sure is that the future is going to be different from what you might imagine. You can get in a lot of trouble by not accepting this simple fact. You can't outrun your shadow, and you can't escape the ripening of karma.

For the time being, anyway, my own teaching programme continued to follow the pattern that Rinpoche had laid down so many years before. Thus, I gave Green Tara initiations in both Los Angeles and Stuttgart and Red Tara and Saraswati in London. I gave White Manjushri in Bristol and the Sky Dharma Menla in Harrogate. As for textual teachings, I taught *The Heart Sutra* in London and Los Angeles. I continued with Rinpoche's *Lamp that Dispels Darkness* in Manchester and completed Sakya Pandita's *Elucidating the Thought of the Sage* in Sakya Changlochen Ling.

Outside of our own centres, I was invited to teach at the Public Course in KIBI held in March. H.H. Karmapa was the principal teacher, giving some explanation from *Entering the Bodhisattva Path*, perhaps his favourite text to teach. He also gave the Bodhisattva Vow and the initiations of Namgyalma and Manjushri Lion Speech from the 9th Karmapa's collection, which he had received in its entirety from Shamar Rinpoche. My part of the programme was an elucidation of *The Short Prayer to Vajradhara*, a famed Kagyu devotional supplication composed by Penkar Jampal Zangpo.

For some time, Karma Thinley Rinpoche had been working on a commentary on *The Seven Points of Mind-Training*. So, when he passed through London, at the end of April, he gave me the reading-transmission for this new work, entitled *Dispelling The Darkness of Suffering*. It contained some special instructions on how to combine the *Mind-Training* teachings with the practice of the deity Chenrezi.

The first major visit of the year happened a couple of weeks later, when H.E. Ratna Vajra Rinpoche arrived in London to teach the *Eight Dream-Like Experiences*, a short work by Jetsun Drakpa Gyaltsen. Alongside this, he gave the initiation of the Three Powerful Wrathful Ones (Vajrapani, Hayagriva and Garuda). Subsequently, in Bristol, Rinpoche bestowed the major initiation of Chakrasamvara from the *Vajramala*, a collection of over forty mandala-initiations brought together by the Indian master, Abhayakaragupta, and now forming part of *The Collection of Tantras*.

As previously, he asked me to teach on the Vajrayana pledges at the conclusion of the initiation. Ten days later, His Eminence visited another of our centres, when he came to Sakya Dechen Ling in Stuttgart. There he gave the major initiation of Chenrezi according to *The*

King's Tradition, a Nyingma cycle of practice derived from the instructions of the seventh-century dharma-king, Songtsen Gampo.

On the morning that Ratna Rinpoche left Stuttgart, I had to rush to the airport to catch a plane to Manchester, as the second major visit of the year was about to start. According to my scheduling, I would arrive two hours earlier than the plane carrying Shamar Rinpoche from France but my flight was delayed, and I arrived in the immigration hall to find Rinpoche already ahead of me in the queue. We emerged together, accompanied by his two attendants, and greeted by the reception-party from Kagyu Ling. Somehow, this slight chaos was just the right start to a marvellous but all too brief visit.

Rinpoche had agreed to my request to teach the commentary on *The Seven Points of Mind-Training*, composed by one of his eminent predecessors, the 5th Shamar, Konchok Yenlak. I knew that Rinpoche especially liked to emphasise *Mind-Training*, and yet he had not previously transmitted this particular text. In the event, it was unforgettable; Rinpoche elegantly wove the Kadam and Kagyu teachings together, giving those present a direct introduction to *Mahamudra*, as he taught the method of meditating on ultimate bodhichitta. Pamela Gayle White later skilfully edited this weekend of teaching in a book entitled *Bringing Mind-Training to Life*, which was published by Rabsel Publications.

Outside of this teaching, Rinpoche was a relaxed, brilliant and warm presence. He particularly enjoyed taking time in the garden of Kagyu Ling, where we could talk together about the issues facing dharma in the West in general and the situation in Karma-Kagyu in particular. Although Rinpoche was completely frank in these conversations, he was free of rancour in his assessment of the political problems of the last thirty years.

Rinpoche also described his vision for Bodhi Path in more detail, and asked me to teach Zhentong Madhyamaka in his American centres there. He told me that he would contact the U.S. Bodhi Path administrators for them to make the necessary arrangements.

I remember feeling, on his last night in Manchester, that, finally, things were suitably aligned for the Kagyu, with H.H. Karmapa and Shamar Rinpoche being in their proper positions. It appeared that the years of struggle were beginning to recede.

A day after leaving Manchester, Shamar Rinpoche had to visit the Diamond Way Centre in London for breakfast and to bestow the reading-transmission of the *Mahamudra* preliminaries. He had insisted we come to this, together with the text required for the transmission. Later that morning, after the reading-transmission there, we waved goodbye to Rinpoche, as he boarded the Eurostar train. He was due to teach at the Bodhi Path Centre in Renchen-Ulm, Germany.

Just over a week later, on the morning of June 11th, we received a phone call telling us that Shamar Rinpoche had suddenly passed away, apparently from heart failure, at breakfast in Renchen-Ulm. He was sixty-one years old. After hastily arranged flights, we arrived there via Strasbourg. H.H. Karmapa flew in, the next morning, from Delhi. Over the days that followed, hundreds of people came to the chapel of rest to see Rinpoche's body laying in state until its transportation to India and, eventually, Kathmandu. It was planned that the cremation would take place there, forty-nine days after Rinpoche's passing.

However, before we could go to Kathmandu and fully assimilate what had just happened, we had important duties in France with the year's third major visit. My master, H.H. Sakya Trizin, had been invited to the Dordogne by the three Nyingma brothers in charge of the Chanteloube Centre – the incarnate-lamas Jigme Khyentse Rinpoche, Tulku Pema Wangyal and Rangdrol Rinpoche – all sons of the late Kangyur Rinpoche. In addition to accepting their invitation, His Holiness had also accepted ours to visit Sakya Changlochen Ling.

At Chanteloube, which is situated quite close to Dhagpo, His Holiness gave teachings on *Parting from the Four Attachments*, the major initiation of Chakrasamvara from the Krishnacharya tradition and the blessing-initiation of Vajrayogini, as well as the initiations of Chenrezi-Mahamudra, Green Tara, Menla and the torma initiation of Kilaya. Four hundred of the brothers' students attended. Due, perhaps, to the large numbers, only the brothers and their immediate family plus our family (at the insistence of His Holiness) were actually able to receive the initiations directly.

As arranged, His Holiness took the time out from this busy programme for a one-day visit to Sakya Changlochen Ling; we invited Jigme Khyentse Rinpoche, together with his wife, Ingrid, and brother, Rangdrol Rinpoche. We had also invited several friends from Dhagpo. His Holiness's first act, on arrival, was to bless the land and buildings. Later on that day, he bestowed the initiation of Manjushri Arapatsana. It seemed particularly appropriate for His Holiness to give this initiation of Sakya's patron deity.

Within two days of this visit from His Holiness, Albena and I flew to Kathmandu to attend Shamar Rinpoche's cremation. It took place over two days at Sharminub, his recently established seat there. Much to my surprise, Matthew Brown from Chicago Bodhi Path approached us to extend an invitation to teach. I had imagined that this would have fallen into abeyance, but, apparently, Shamar Rinpoche had found the time to let them know his wishes.

From there, it was straight back to France, where I gave a three-day teaching on the *Three Vows* at Dhagpo. Immediately afterwards, I concluded the course on *Elucidating The Thought of the Sage*, and led a retreat upon Gonkar at Sakya Changlochen Ling. The next month, I taught Tokme Zangpo's commentary on *The Seven Points of Mind-Training* at Fundaçion Sakya in southern Spain, where I had been invited by the new resident lama, Rinchen Gyaltsen. At the time, I didn't realise how frequently I would be requested to give this teaching over the next two years.

Two months later, we were back in California. Initially, I gave Chenrezi-Mahamudra initiation and the *Eight Verses of Mind-Training* at Sakya Samten Ling. We then drove up the coast to Santa Barbara, where we stayed with Bart and Suzan Mandel, two disciples of the late Trungpa Rinpoche, who had become part of Bodhi Path. While there, I gave some teachings on *Parting from the Four Attachments* at the request of the local Bodhi Path Centre. Santa Barbara itself turned out to be a lovely place – an old mission town that was, once upon a time, going to be the movie capital of the world before the circus moved down to Hollywood. Behind it are the dry Santa Ynez mountains, and, in front of it, is the blue endless Pacific, stretching all the way to Japan.

From there, we headed up Highway 5 to San Francisco and Berkeley, where I taught Tokme Zangpo's *Seven*

Points of Mind-Training at Ewam Choden. It was enjoyable to be in the Bay Area again, a place where so many great movies reverberate in your mind. I always liked San Francisco.

As it happened, at the beginning of December, we were on the other side of the Pacific Ocean, in Japan, for the Sixth Supreme Buddhist Summit. It was hosted again at the Royal Grand Hall of Buddhism. It's a time of year that can be bone-chilling in Japan, even without snow. So it was something of a relief to go from there back to California, where I gave Green Tara at Sakya Samten Ling.

2015 began in a sombre manner for our dharma community with the death of Rana Lister. Born in a traditional Jewish family with roots in Poland, she had given her life to the practice of dharma. Perhaps her major contribution lay in the artwork she provided for the books and translations issued by Ganesha Press. Three generations of her family are now part of our community.

The passing of years, evident in the flow of the generations, one handing on to another, is itself the sweet sad music of impermanence. For us, it's where the truth shows its face, a beauty that is unmoved by our wishes but one proclaiming that the only way to the timeless is through the moments of time themselves, as Mr Eliot must have meant when he said:

Only through time time is conquered.[6]

Shortly after Rana's funeral, I travelled to Stuttgart to give Shakyashri's White Tara and Tokme Zangpo's *Seven Points of Mind-Training*. I would continue this teaching in two further visits that year, together with the initiations of Chenrezi and Menla. From Germany we went to KIBI, having just received the news from California of the birth of our grand-daughter, Clio. Although KIBI had also asked me to teach *Mind-Training*, in this case Khenpo Mriti, who was in charge of the programme in those days, asked me to employ the commentary of Shamar Konchok Yenlak. It seems that, as I had just received it the previous year from Shamar Rinpoche himself, people were anxious to receive that rare transmission.

During that same week, H.H. Karmapa gave the initiations of Choling's Vajrasattva and Chenrezi from the 9th Karmapa's collection. Following this course, Albena and I travelled up to Rajpur. There, H.H. Sakya Trizin gave the medium-length initiation of White Tara, known as *The Innermost Drop of the Noble Lady of Immortality*. It is a cycle that originated with the great Jamyang Khyentse Wangpo and is preserved in *The Treasury of Revealed Teachings*.

Our next trip was to California in April. After giving the initiation of Manjushri Arapatsana in Sakya Samten Ling, we visited three Bodhi Path centres in succession, travelling northwards, first to San Luis Obispo. It's a pretty spot, nestling in a cluster of green hills, about four or five hours drive from Los Angeles. The countryside around reminded me a little of Devon; some spells of enchantment have been cast here in the past. The city's name reflects the fact that, like so much else around, it was founded by the Spanish coming up from Mexico and still bears architectural traces of those beginnings. I gave two days' teaching on Madhyamaka, which reflected somewhat the topic that Shamar Rinpoche had actually wanted me to teach in his centres. However, subsequently, in the centres in Santa Barbara and Pasadena, they preferred that I teach Konchok Yenlak's commentary on *The Seven Points of Mind-Training*.

I would return to complete the *Mind-Training* teachings in Santa Barbara in July. On the way, I stopped over in Chicago to teach Madhyamaka in the Bodhi Path Centre there. Thankfully, Chicago was not too hot for the time of year, and we got to appreciate its down-town and lake-front. It would only be on a later visit that we'd go to a blues club there and would hear the music that had travelled all the way up Highway 61. I remember thinking then that Chicago must have seemed a long way to those great Delta musicians, when the thunder was rolling over Clarksdale, and the levee was about to break.

This was not my last visit to Bodhi Path that year. In the autumn we made an East Coast tour. It commenced in Washington D.C., one of the most stately of capital cities. While there, I was once again asked to teach *The Seven Points of Mind-Training*. From Washington we took a slow train to deep Virginia, where Bodhi Path has its main American centre, near Natural Bridge. It's quite close to the university town of Lexington and really quite an other-wordly part of the South.

Shamar Rinpoche had, it appears, truly loved the place and had built a house there, close to the wooden meditation-hall and the Stupa that he had constructed. There was a small community of members living on site, including the French dharma-teacher Tsony, one of several teachers who work for the Bodhi Path in the U.S.A. The glowing reds and browns of the autumn woods around the meditation-hall made a blazing backdrop to the teachings.

One lunchtime we went out for hamburgers in a local joint. It was more of a one-room country shack than anything else, but very popular with the local people. It was a great place – straight out of the old weird America.

I could hear The Stanley Brothers singing 'Rank Strangers' in the background, and looked around at the faces of the people – hard times were etched in some of the older ones' faces, but kindness too. They are mocked by the professors I'd heard chirping and chattering in Manhattan hotels, and, right now, the dharma's not reaching them much. I hope some day that changes.

I taught on Madhyamaka there, and then we left for New York, where the Bodhi Path uses a space in a brownstone on the Upper East Side of Manhattan, provided by the dharma-patron, Elise Frick. For that group, I gave Geshe Langri Thangpa's *Eight Verses of Mind-Training*.

Our final destination was the fabled island of Martha's Vineyard, a summer playground of politicians, the well-connected and the occasional hungry shark, some two hours from Boston. Its impeccable rustic tastefulness mixed with a little hint of Captain Ahab gave it an atmosphere that was noticeably different from the easy-going warmth of the South or the cool excitement of Manhattan. There, in the beautiful Bodhi Path meditation-hall, I taught Konchok Yenlak's *Seven Points of Mind-Training* once again.

It had been quite an introduction to the Bodhi Path in America and to something of the wider dharma scene there. Previously, we had only seen Los Angeles and San Francisco. Now we had visited eight further groups. It had become obvious to me that, to launch Bodhi Path, Shamar Rinpoche had deliberately pitched it as a non-sectarian organisation, placing relatively little emphasis on Vajrayana, the Karma-Kagyu tradition, or, indeed, his own position within Kagyu hierarchy and Tibetan history. This observation tied in with what Shamar Rinpoche himself had said to me a few years previously.

As for teaching dharma in general in the U.S.A. – after some time, I had to re-think things. In fact, it was about this point that I realised that a lot of hard work is required from a lot of people to ensure the flourishing of the dharma in America – but once you start on something, you can't just walk away.

As Shantideva declared:

> Having made the commitment,
> If I do not fulfil it,
> Then, since I have deceived all sentient beings
> What kind of rebirth will I take?[7]

In between these various trips to Bodhi Path centres, I was able to visit Sakya Dolma Ling in May, to give the initiations of Chenrezi and White Tara, together with Ngawang Legdrup's guiding instructions. For newer people, there, I taught *Parting from the Four Attachments*.

In late July and August, we were in the Dordogne. H.H Karmapa arrived at Dhagpo on the 24th of July, and, despite suffering from an atrocious cold, proceeded to give the Bodhisattva Vow and Chenrezi initiation. As usual, he taught in his flawless English and was translated into French by Thinley Tulku, the American-French incarnation recognised by the 16th Karmapa and Kalu Rinpoche. Two weeks later, my own programme started in the Dhagpo Institute, with two days for the general public, followed by three days on Tsarchen's commentary on the *Fifty Verses on the Lama*. Such a two-part programme would be the regular shape of my summer teaching at Dhagpo from then on.

Our own summer course in Sakya Changlochen Ling, just ten miles away, was also in two parts: an initial week, in which I started on Sonam Tsemo's *General Presentation of the Tantra Sets*, and a second week dedicated to the initiation and guiding instructions of White Tara. I would continue with Sonam Tsemo's text for the next two summer courses at Changlochen, accompanying it with White Tara and Vajrapani retreats.

Although the year had been full of travel, we managed to maintain the programme of teachings at the centres in England. I gave the initiations of Manjushri Arapatsana, Vasudhara, the goddess of prosperity, and the form of Shakyamuni Buddha known as Vajrasana, all three being from the lineage of Bari, as well as the Sky Dharma Chenrezi and Amitabha, and Shakyashri's Green Tara. In addition to these teachings, at Kagyu Ling, I began to teach the 3rd Karmapa's *Showing the Buddha-Nature* with Jamgon Kongtrul's commentary, *Clarifying the Thought of Rangjung*. It would stretch well into the following year.

Finally, Christmas saw us once again in Los Angeles, where I gave the initiation of Chenrezi at our centre. Just two weeks later, we were on the other side of the globe, in Hong Kong, being hosted by Ivy and Kitty Lai's family, stalwart supporters of Shamar Rinpoche. The Bodhi Path Centre there had requested me to teach *The Short Prayer to Vajradhara* over three days. The next stop was Sakya Dechen Ling in Stuttgart, where I taught *Parting from the Four Attachments* and gave the initiation of Manjushri Arapatsana. I would return there twice more that year, to give the initiations of Yellow Dzambhala and Shakyashri's White Tara and some Kadam teachings.

It was 2016 now, and ten years since the publication of *Rain of Clarity*. For the next two years, I would teach it consecutively in Bristol and London, as well as in Los Angeles. It had been intended as a bridge to the detailed and profound teachings of our traditional texts such as those of Sakya Pandita, Sonam Tsemo and Gorampa Sonam Sengge. It also was designed as a resource for those students who had some teaching responsibilities in our centres.

In these Sakya places, I also gave the initiations of White Manjushri, Red Tara, Menla, Atisha's Green Tara and Chenrezi-Mahamudra. In our Kagyu centres, I gave the initiations of Namgyalma from the 9th Karmapa's collection, Yellow Dzambhala, Choling's Vajrasattva and Vajrakilaya and the One Thousand-Armed Chenrezi, as well as two Zhentong texts – *The Correct Analysis of the Zhentong Madhyamaka* by Karmapa Mikyo Dorje, and Jamgon Kongtrul's *Rays of the Vajra Moon*, both of which Rinpoche had given me in Toronto over thirty years previously.

Teaching these two, one after the other, was quite unusual. In fact, although Jamgon Kongtrul was unambiguously a proponent of the Zhentong perspective, and had done much to ensure its survival as a system, Mikyo Dorje's position was more complex, as he had actually criticised the Zhentong view in some places. Many years ago, Rinpoche told me that it was his understanding that Mikyo Dorje skilfully varied his presentation on Madhyamaka in accord with the philosophical orientations of his disciples.

That year, I taught in three particular European Kagyu centres for the first time. Thus, at the end of April, I gave general dharma teaching in Espace Bouddhiste Tibetain in Paris, a part of the Dhagpo mandala of centres, and in Karma Euzer Ling, in Normandy. This centre was also the location of Rabsel Publications, a major French Buddhist publisher, who had already brought out a French edition of *Rain of Clarity*.

The centre in Paris is next door to Père Lachaise cemetery, where we were able to take some photographs at Apollinaire's grave. I wasn't sure that they would be any good, and then remembered somebody telling me that dignity's never been photographed, and smiled to myself.

In September, I was invited to teach at the Bodhi Path Centre in Renchen-Ulm, the site of Shamar Rinpoche's passing. Established by his long-time disciple Sabine Teubner, it is the principal centre of Bodhi Path in Europe. Being located in a corner of Germany close to both France and Switzerland, it is perfectly situated for such a role.

As with the previous years, we spent quite some time in North America that year. My first tour was one month long, from late March to late April. It began in Berkeley, where I completed the teachings on the *Seven Points of Mind-Training*. From there, we drove down the Pacific Coastal Highway to San Luis Obispo, where I taught *The Short Prayer to Vajradhara*, and then to Santa Barbara, for teaching on the Madhyamaka View. In Los Angeles, I taught *The Short Prayer to Vajradhara* for Bodhi Path Pasadena, and bestowed the Black Manjushri initiation for Sakya Samten Ling.

Finally, I flew up to Canada. It was certainly something of a shock to go from the spring weather of Southern California to a still snow-covered Calgary. Perhaps the challenging weather made it appropriate for me to teach the *Mind-Training* of the 5th Shamarpa once again, since this system places a major emphasis on the transformation of difficulties into the spiritual path.

Being in Calgary was auspicious because Karma Thinley Rinpoche had a small centre there. Three decades ago, with the aid of his Swiss-Canadian disciple, Jetsunma Rigzin Khandro, he had established Marpa Gompa. Jetsunma and some of her centre's members attended the *Mind-Training* teaching, and, before I left for London, they requested me to visit the centre, an invitation that I was very happy to accept.

We had then to return to England briefly, as Rinpoche himself was due to arrive from Toronto. I was able to receive the transmission for Rangjung Dorje's text entitled *Direct Introduction to the Three Kayas*, a *Mahamudra*-related text. Rinpoche also gave the reading-transmission for the long Chenrezi Fasting Ritual text authored by Jamgon Kongtrul.

Immediately following Rinpoche's departure for Nepal, we travelled to Madrid. H.H. Sakya Trizin was there to give teachings on *Parting from the Four Attachments* and the initiation of Chenrezi-Mahamudra. Albena and I stayed in the smart district of Salamanca and enjoyed a delightful three days spending some time with His Holiness in one of the grand cities of Europe.

From there, it was straight to Mexico for my annual programme, and to hear Spanish spoken with a rather different accent. Year on year, Sakya Dolma Ling was developing steadily due to the commitment of students. To a certain degree, dharma in Mexico is confined to the affluent in society, but fortunately our sangha, although benefitting from a few very generous patrons, is somewhat more mixed.

It's also noticeable that the Mexican Catholic background of those who come to the dharma tends to foster a sense of piety that is, in some senses, more akin to traditional dharma attitudes than the suspicion of religious forms familiar from the U.S.A. and U.K. One example of this is the ease with which those who have been brought up with devotion to the Virgin of Guadalupe develop devotion to Tara when they become Buddhists. However, this same strongly Catholic background can also impede people's commitment to dharma through social and familial pressure to remain Catholic and thus 'Mexican'.

On this occasion, the focal part of my teaching was the initiation of Bhutadamara. I gave this together with Zhuchen Tsultrim Rinchen's guiding instructions on the practice. I also fitted the initiation of Green Tara and teachings on the *Heart Sutra* into the week-long programme.

Happily enough, despite this busy schedule, I found the time for some extra retreat that year. So, in accord with H.H. Karmapa's suggestion, I accomplished four weeks' retreat on Hevajra and then a further week on Vajrayogini before the end of the year. There's always some new face of practice to show itself at such times. Maybe it's always been there, but you need the retreat to be quiet enough to see it. It's the same with all our dharma endeavours – the great bliss of awakening to the true nature is all that is necessary, but it's necessary to have the time to find your way back to it. This, above all, is the meaning of practice and retreat.

The first three weeks of August were spent in France. The Dhagpo administration had requested extensive teachings on *The Fourteen Root Downfalls*. In response, I taught Jetsun Drakpa Gyaltsen's *Dispelling Error*, which I had received from Phende Rinpoche over three decades earlier. As I had only taught it once before, some students came from England to join this course. After a further two weeks spent in Sakya Changlochen Ling, we flew to India, taking Katharina with us, to see H.H Sakya Trizin. She had not been to the Phodrang since she was six months old.

I had requested His Holiness to bestow a series of initiations of wealth-deities from *A Collection of Sadhanas*. In all, His Holiness bestowed nine initiations, together with their reading-transmissions. Included in this series were five forms of Dzambhala: White Dzambhala from the Atisha tradition, Green Dzambhala according to Kalachakra Tantra, Yellow Dzambhala according to the Guhyasamaja Tantra, Black Dzambhala from the tradition of Shakyashri and a second Black Dzambhala from the *Ocean of Sadhanas*. Additionally there were two Vasudharas: White Vasudhara from the Atisha tradition and Yellow Vasudhara from the Jamari tradition. Finally, there were two forms of Ganapati: White Ganapati and Ganapati in a mandala of four deities, both from the lineage of Atisha.

While at the Phodrang, we had the opportunity to talk with His Holiness and Gyal Yum Chenmo-la, as well as Ratna Vajra Rinpoche and his wife, Dagmo Kalden-la, about the recently announced changes concerning the office of the Sakya Trizin itself. These would result in His Holiness being the first Sakya Trizin to step down from that position. His Holiness told us that the suggestion made by Jamyang Khyentse Wangpo, back in the nineteenth century, that Sakya itself should adopt the Ngor branch's custom of rotating the senior position in the sub-school every three years, had influenced his decision on this matter. We confirmed that we would attend the enthronement of H.E. Ratna Vajra Rinpoche that had been scheduled for the following spring.

That autumn saw my second American tour of the year for Bodhi Path. It was confined mainly to the East Coast. It began in Martha's Vineyard, where I gave some teachings on Madhyamaka. Subsequently, I travelled down to New York to teach Tokme Zangpo's *Thirty-Seven Prac-*

tices. From there I flew to Roanoke in south-western Virginia, the nearest airport to Natural Bridge, where I taught Konchok Yenlak's commentary on *The Seven Points of Mind-Training.* I went northwards then to Washington, on this occasion being hosted by Ed and Huei-ling Worthy, two long-term disciples of Shamar Rinpoche. The topic for the teaching in that city was *The Seven Points of Mind-Training,* as it was on the final stop of this tour, when I returned to Chicago.

There were two new Bodhi Path centres in Europe on my itinerary in 2017. February saw us in the beautiful Spanish coastal city of Valencia; I gave some teaching on Buddha-nature and a lecture at the local University to clarify the Buddhist understanding of mindfulness. Later that year, in the autumn, I began teaching *The Rays of the Vajra Moon* for the group in Prague, a city which gave the world Franz Kafka, a great author who never goes out of date. I would also teach Jamgon Kongtrul's text in Renchen-Ulm and Manchester that year.

For our two Sakya centres in England, I gave Gonkar and the Lords of the Three Families, and, from the Bari collection, Chenrezi in the form of Simhanada, the goddess Prajnaparamita and Hayagriva, this last deity for dispelling obstacles. At Sakya Dechen Ling in Stuttgart, I began to teach Ngorchen Konchok Lhundrup's *The Three Visions* and gave the initiations of Bari's Namgyalma, Atisha's Green Tara and Amitayus. In our Kagyu centres, I bestowed the initiations of Menla, Amitayus, Green Tara, Lion Speech Manjushri and Milarepa.

At the beginning of March, Albena and I attended the enthronement of Ratna Vajra Rinpoche as the 42nd Sakya Trizin. It took place at the Sakya monastery in the settlement of Puruwala, some fifty miles from Dehra Dun. It was a place that I had last visited over thirty years previously to stay with His Holiness the 41st and his then young family.[8] It was rather moving to see Rinpoche enthroned there, where we had played cricket three decades earlier. Having known Rinpoche since he was three years old, I was completely confident that he would be a great holder of the throne.

On the way back through Delhi, we had lunch with H.H. Karmapa in Delhi. He was very happy as usual. However, it seemed as though he had something to tell us but had judged that it wasn't quite the time to do so. Just two weeks or so later, His Holiness made the announcement of his marriage to Sang Yum-la Rinchen Yangzom. We could not have been more delighted.

Following this, we flew to Los Angeles, where I gave Gonkar and Namgyalma, followed by a visit to Sakya Dolma Ling, where I taught our Mexican sangha the *Thirty-Seven Practices* and gave the initiations of Chenrezi-Mahamudra, Green Tara and Red Tara, concluding with the initiation of Sakya Pandita.

Back in London, we hosted Karma Thinley Rinpoche, who gave me the transmission of Karmapa Thegchog Dorje's commentary on the 3rd Karmapa's *Direct Introduction to the Three Kayas*, as well as a ritual that he himself had composed for averting obstacles. Since Sakya Dechen Ling had just moved into a new location in Notting Hill, Rinpoche visited to bless it. For the fortunate students who attended, he also gave the reading-transmission of *The Heart Sutra*.

It was the first year that we visited Karma Migyur Ling, a centre in the foothills of the Alps and one of the major dharma centres in France. I was there to teach *The Short Prayer to Vajradhara*. The centre has been guided for over forty years by Lama Teunsang from Nangchen, a disciple of the 16th Karmapa and Kalu Rinpoche. Assisted only by his loyal French disciples and his own determination and devotion, he has built a traditional temple, a retreat centre and eight stupas on the side of a steep hill. Appropriately enough, this hill-side enclave possesses a wonderful outlook over the French countryside spread below.

It was May when we flew there, via Geneva, where I gave a public talk for the local Kagyu group directed by Agathe Chevalier and her husband, Jean-Marc Falcombello. As for that city itself – it seemed to me that Jean Calvin's influence in the sixteenth century had predestined it to be a somewhat repressed place with no icons, no feasts and little to do but make money, invent the Protestant Work Ethic, give birth to modern capitalism and, via Rousseau, the city's second most famous inhabitant, foster revolutionary fanaticism and bloodshed. Quite a legacy!

It was tight scheduling but we just managed to get back to England in time to greet Ratna Rinpoche, now H.H. the 42nd Sakya Trizin, on his first visit as Throne Holder. In Bristol, he bestowed the major initiation of Sangye Menla from the kriya tantra section of *The Collection of Tantras*, after giving a very well-attended public lecture.

Privately, I received the guiding instruction for Chenrezi practice in the King's Lineage, which followed from the initiation that he had bestowed in Stuttgart three years previously. Later that week, His Holiness came to stay with us in London, where he blessed the new Sakya Dechen Ling, and, the following evening, gave the initiation of The Three Powerful and Wrathful Ones.

Luckily there was also time to take His Holiness to Lords for a day of cricket. It was a county match between Middlesex and Surrey, and it provided a most relaxing time in a truly English setting. Before His Holiness departed, we discussed plans for his visit to the U.S.A. scheduled for the next summer and his imminent visit to Sakya Changlochen Ling. His Holiness's stay in the Dordogne would be shared with Chanteloube, as with his father's visit three years earlier. When the visit took place, he gave the torma initiation of Vajrakilaya, and blessed a spot as a site on which a stupa should be constructed in the future.

By this time, our centre in the Dordogne had grown greatly from the early years, both in land and in buildings. Of course, the whole area around us is a powerful place for dharma-activity. The landscape is a harmonious balance of hills, rivers and forest, as if all the elements that support life have gathered through the long centuries of dependent-origination; the castles and manors that dot the land seem to echo still to the Occitan songs of past troubadours. All in all, it makes it a suitable location for grand institutions of dharma.

For some time, I had been working on a new book entitled *Wisdom in Exile*. It drew on some of the articles that I had contributed over the years to Tricycle, highlighting issues involved in the transmission of dharma to the West. Both H.H. Sakya Trichen and H.H. Karmapa kindly contributed forewords, as did Rinpoche. So, for a couple of months that summer, there was a flurry of activity around this book. Ganesha Press brought it out in June of that year, and Rabsel Editions published the French edition a couple of months later. Sakya Dechen Ling hosted the London launch party, and, the same week, I travelled to Paris to discuss it on Sagesse Bouddhiste, the weekly television show dedicated to Buddhism on France 2. There was also a U.S. launch for the book early in July hosted by Sakya Samten Ling and one held in Paris by Rabsel Editions in September.

While I was there in California, I also gave Sangye Menla initiation in Los Angeles and, travelling up to Berkeley, gave a course on shamatha and vipashyana meditation as they are taught in *The Triple Vision* at Ewam Choden.

August was then spent in the Dordogne, continuing with *The Root Downfalls* at Dhagpo and *The General Presentation of the Tantra Sets* at Changlochen. The conclusion of this teaching coincided with a brief visit to Dhagpo Kundreul Ling by H.H. Karmapa. So we went to pay our respects. In fact, on our return to London, the young French incarnation of the late Gendun Rinpoche from Kundreul Ling, was going to stay with us for a few weeks. It had been arranged, after His Holiness's suggestion to us over lunch, to help him settle in before his courses at London University started.

Thartse Shabdrung Rinpoche passed through London in late September, on the way to France. At my request, he gave the initiation of Sangye Menla at Sakya Dechen Ling.

There would be two trips to Asia that autumn. The first was to attend the Buddhist Summit in Colombo, hosted jointly by Nembutsu-shu and the Sri Lankan Government. It took place in early November, and the time was split between the actual conference itself and a subsequent three days sight-seeing tour of the country's most important Buddhist sites.

The days given over to the conference were marked by a great seriousness. In the end, it seemed that all the delegates from over fifty participating countries had articulated concerns for the survival and flourishing of dharma that were common to all. One particular issue that has emerged at this and other summits is the relative poverty of much of the Buddhist world, and Buddhism's resulting inability to defend itself from the corrosive down-sides of modernity and the activities of predatory missionary groups. This latter problem is evident, for instance, in Mongolia, where the effort to rebuild dharma there, after the six-decade-long Communist persecution, is being undercut by wealthy Christian missionary groups from the U.S.A. and South Korea, who can spend freely in their recruitment campaigns. We heard much about this and similar issues from elsewhere, including from small Buddhist communities in Africa.

The Sri Lankan authorities invested heavily in this summit, and much of the political leadership of Sri Lanka attended, underscoring the important symbolic role that dharma plays in the culture of the nation there. Naturally enough, there was a very weighty Sri Lankan monastic contingent present. I wondered if it might be possible to ask them about Abhayagiri, the monastic complex that had been doctrinally Mahayana in the mediaeval period, while remaining Theravada in its monastic lineage. Regrettably, the opportunity never arose. It's a pity – it would have been something of an ecumenical matter.

The three days that were allotted to visiting important religious and cultural spots left strong impressions, mentally and physically. As our chartered buses trundled painfully from one 'meet and greet' to another, staged in such places as Anuradhapura and Kandy, there was ample opportunity to reflect on turning difficulties into the spiritual path.

Coach journeys apart, Sri Lanka itself, seemed quite a friendly place, perhaps because of the strong emphasis on moral training in the culture, but, at the same time, the gulf between the ordained sangha and other Buddhists appeared to be causing a slide away from the dharma. In fact, it was noticeable that one of the most popular monks with the educated Sri Lankan middle-class is a Westerner, Ajahn Brahmavamso. He is particularly appreciated there for his intelligent but traditional presentation of dharma and his approachable manner.

Ajahn Brahm, an Englishman who was trained in the Thai Forest tradition and currently directs a Theravada monastery in Western Australia, was in fact along for this trip in his capacity as the Australian delegate to the Supreme Buddhist Summit. He always has something interesting to say and is a real force for the growth of dharma.

Having seen a cutting from the original Bodhi Tree during this time in Sri Lanka, a month later we saw the site of the original tree in Bodh Gaya, the holiest of places in our dharma world. We had journeyed to the Indian province of Bihar to attend the International Karma Kagyu Meeting, held in the presence of H.H. Karmapa. It was scheduled just before the annual Kagyu Monlam was due to take place there. I had been asked to speak on the situation of dharma in the West. About one hundred people had been invited – mostly Tibetan and with a reasonable number of Westerners. My speech was translated into Tibetan by Sabchu Rinpoche, who is presently in charge of Swayambhu monastery in Kathmandu. Outside of the conference we had some time with His Holiness and his wife Sangyum-la, congratulating them on their wedding.

A day after returning to London, I flew to Los Angeles with Katharina; Albena stayed behind to do some retreat. Overcoming jet-lag, I gave Atisha's White Dzambhala initiation before returning to London to celebrate the New Year and the birth of our new grandson, Hector, to Michael and his wife, Victoria.

Three weeks later, in Bristol, I taught Rinpoche's *Telescope of Faith* and gave the initiation of Black Manjushri. I would return to Bristol to finish this textual teaching in early June. Teachings in Stuttgart and Valencia quickly followed, and, then, in Manchester, I continued with *Pointing a Finger at the Dharmakaya* from the preceding year. I would make a further visit in July to complete this, the shortest work in the famed *Mahamudra* trilogy of the 9th Karmapa.

In March, I journeyed to the Dhagpo Mandala Centre in Mohra in eastern Germany to teach *The Rays of the Vajra Moon*. The centre is staffed by Lama Yeshe Zangmo and her dedicated team, who were mostly trained in Dhagpo Kundreul Ling. The centre is actually located in the Thuringian village, where Martin Luther, accidental father of modernity, was born in 1483.

After giving White Dzambhala in London, we flew to California and returned to the Bodhi Path centres in Santa Barbara and San Luis Obispo, teaching *The Rays of the Vajra Moon* and the *Four Dharmas of Gampopa*. In Sakya Samten Ling, I gave Green Tara initiation, before flying up to a frozen Calgary, where I again taught *The Rays of The Vajra Moon*.

A brief intermission in England, during which I began to teach Gampopa's *Precious Rosary of the Supreme Path* in Harrogate, was followed within a month by a return to Los Angeles. H.H. Ratna Vajra, the 42nd Sakya Trizin, was coming to Los Angeles as part of of his U.S. tour. On this first visit by a Khon lineage holder to our centre, His Holiness gave the initiation of Padmasambhava revealed by Apham Terton, a master widely regarded as the previous incarnation of H.H. the present 41ˢᵗ Sakya Trichen.

The next day we flew to Mexico City. We had to be there in time to welcome His Holiness and party, who followed on a little later. It was seven years since his father, the 41ˢᵗ Sakya Trichen, had visited, so the Sakya Dolma Ling members were overjoyed. The recently acquired home of our centre is in the pleasant and somewhat 'arty' district of Coyoacan, the place where Hernan Cortes established his base before the final Conquest of Moctezuma's Mexico in the early sixteenth century and a place of galleries, museums and grand houses. It provided a suitably historic setting for His Holiness's teachings. While he was with us, His Holiness bestowed the initiations of the Three Powerful Ones and White Saraswati, and also taught the epistolary text, *A Garland of Jewels*, a work composed by his Khon predecessor Chogyal Phakpa in the thirteenth century, for one of his Mongol patrons.

His Holiness talked to me about his dedication to maintaining the standards of dharma education in the monasteries in India and Nepal and his plans to oversee new editions of all the ritual texts to aid this. He also wanted to discuss how best we can communicate the dharma view of abortion and non-violence to new students in the West.[9] After the departure of His Holiness to the U.S.A., I gave the initiation of White Dzambhala, which I had received from his father two years earlier.

I had three European trips to make in quick succession on my return from North America. In Karma Migyur Ling, I taught *The Four Limitless Meditations*, and in

Stuttgart I continued with *The Three Visions*. The third trip involved a visit to a new Bodhi Path destination – Stavanger in Norway, a fishing town, which, like the country itself, has boomed in recent years due to off-shore oil exploration. There, I taught *The Rays of the Vajra Moon* once again, although as it was mid-June in the land of the midnight sun, there was not much time for the moon to appear while I was there.

In July we returned again to Los Angeles, where we had the great joy of welcoming my master, H.H. the 41st Sakya Trichen to Sakya Samten Ling. His Holiness had only two days to teach in Los Angeles. The first day he taught for the Sakya centre in Hacienda Heights, affiliated to Tsechen Kunchab Ling. There, he gave the initiation of Sitatapatra from *One Hundred Initiations of Narthang*, together with some instructions for meditation on Amitabha at the time of death composed by Sakya Pandita. The following day, we hosted him in Santa Monica, where he taught *Parting from The Four Attachments* and gave the initiation of White Saraswati. Before His Holiness left, we made arrangements to see him in the autumn, during my next tour of Bodhi Path centres.

Within a few days, we were six thousand miles away, in Dhagpo, where I completed the teachings on *The Fourteen Root Downfalls*. In Changlochen, I gave the initiations of the Twenty-One Taras from the Atisha lineage. As we did it in a fairly leisurely manner, it took twelve days to complete, but it was the biggest collection that I had given.

In September, I made a short German tour, taking in Renchen-Ulm and Stuttgart and a new venue, the Bodhi Path Centre in the city of Bregenz, just over the border in Austria. There, I taught *The Eight Verses of Mind-Training*. The city itself is impressively located at the end of the Lake of Constance and close to the Alps.

After visiting Bristol to give the Chenrezi-Maham-udra initiation, we arrived in New York on the 8th of October. Our first step was lunch with His Holiness and Gyal Yum Chenmo-la in Walden, and then, after a couple of days spent in the Village, we flew down to Virginia for a weekend of teaching at Natural Bridge. The topic was the *Four Dharmas*, and the autumn weather was mild. From Roanoke, we flew west to Chicago. There, I taught Tokme Zangpo's *Thirty-Seven Practices*, and then flew back eastwards to Washington D.C., where once again I taught *The Seven Points of Mind-Training*.

The texts that I was asked to teach in the Bodhi Path centres made me reflect a little on the difference between Vajrayana and non-Vajrayana modes of teaching. In teaching Mahayana texts, such as *Mind-Training*, one is drawing on one's knowledge, a knowledge acquired from one's own studies with teachers, to make a connection for people between their present situation and the help that the dharma represents. One's role is essentially that of a spiritual friend. Yet it's quite different in Vajrayana. There, the master who bestows the initiations, which are the only means of entering Vajrayana, has, in a sense, to disappear so that the necessary connections can be made in the initiation between the students' present state of being and the enlightened energies of the deity into whose practice they are being initiated.

Due to this, the Vajrayana teacher has to draw upon the reservoir of his own accomplishment gained during previous retreats and replenished by ongoing and unbroken practice. He is not just a spiritual friend but a conduit to the mandala of the deities. Thus the demands upon the Vajrayana teacher are much greater in terms of maintenance of the requisite vows and practice, as is spelled out in the tantras and related treatises.

Since Rinpoche first gave me some authority in Vajrayana, I've been going back and forth between these two modes. It seems to be what is required nowadays, as people need to be tutored in the basic teachings, and then, as they commit to serious practice, they must receive the necessary Vajrayana teachings.

There were two further teachings in England that year: London, where I gave Manjushri Arapatsana and the *Eight Verses of Mind-Training*, and Manchester, where I began the *Jewel Ornament of Liberation*. It would be the fourth time that I would teach this major text at Kagyu Ling.

In between these two, we visited Prague, where I continued with *The Rays of the Vajra Moon*. During this visit, we learned more of the situation for dharma in the Czech Republic. It seems that, even during the years of Communist suppression of religion, there had been a measure of small-scale dharma activity, some of which was connected with the eccentric Swabian artist and guru, Anagarika Govinda. However, since the country's liberation from Communism in 1989, the Diamond Way has become the biggest dharma presence. In fact, Prague Bodhi Path itself consists largely of former members of Diamond Way – a pattern that is reduplicated in most of their groups in Europe.

In early December, we attended the Karma-Kagyu International Meeting for a second time. I had been asked to lecture on connections between the Kagyu and the other traditions. Immediately before we left Bodhgaya, we had lunch with H.H. Karmapa. Among the topics of conversation was his recent meeting with Karmapa Orgyen Thinley in France, who, as is evident, shares His Holiness's profound concern for the future of the Kagyu tradition. This connection between the two must be judged a very positive sign for the future, as is the birth of a son, Thugsey-la, to His Holiness and Sangyum-la.

Back in London, we had just landed when Karma Thinley Rinpoche arrived from Kathmandu for his usual rest before travelling on to Toronto. During this couple of days with us, Rinpoche gave the reading-transmission for a commentary that he had recently composed on the *Three Heaps Sutra*. He also found the time to give the famous *Calling the Lama from Afar*, composed by Jamgon Kongtrul.

Chapter Ten
Good Enough for Now

Sometimes in life you're rolling through stormy weather, and other times the sea is calm. Sometimes your ship's been split to splinters, while there are days when you might even feel like you're simply sailing into a world of mystery.

As for me, the waves of karma carried me next to Los Angeles, in early January 2019. I was there to bestow the Green Tara initiation at our centre there. Later that same month, I gave White Ganapati initiation in Bristol and then flew to Stuttgart, to give further teaching on *The Three Visions* and the initiation of Menla. Finally, I was in Valencia to teach the *Four Dharmas of Gampopa*.

After some further teaching on the *Jewel Ornament* in Kagyu Ling and *Mind-Training* in London, we travelled to Paris in March. Rabsel Editions had just published *Arabesques dans la Vacuité*, the French edition of my new work, *Patterns in Emptiness*. It had been translated by Audrey Desserrières, my very able interpreter from Dhagpo. An evening at Espace Bouddhiste Tibétain was dedicated to this new publication, followed by a weekend on *Madhyamaka* in Karma Euzer Ling in Normandy. It's a very different landscape there from the Dordogne, with which we have grown so familiar over the years. I have the feeling that Normandy, as its name and history suggest, is already Northern Europe; Dordogne and its Romanesque city, Périgueux, on the other hand, seem to be the South.

The end of the month saw me in Möhra, continuing with the *Rays of the Vajra Moon*, and then, more or less immediately, we flew to Mexico. The week there was spent teaching the *Eight Verses of Mind-Training* and giving the initiations of Green Tara and Chenrezi. Mexico City was followed by Los Angeles, where I gave the initiation of White Tara and Ngawang Legdrup's guiding instructions, as well as some brief teaching on *Parting from the Four Attachments*.

After a week in London, we were in Warsaw for the first time in seventeen years. The city looked wealthier than before. I had been invited by the recently established Khyenkong Centre there. This centre had been founded under the direction of Beru Khyentse Rinpoche and his son, the 4th Jamgon Kongtrul, two of the most eminent masters of the Karma-Kagyu tradition, and so I was very happy to accept this invitation. It had been set up by a couple, Elvira and Kris, long-time disciples of Khyentse Rinpoche. My principal teaching on this first visit was *The Jewel Ornament of Liberation*. In fact, I recalled that Karma Thinley Rinpoche had once mentioned Beru Khyentse's own mastery of this text, so it seemed an appropriate choice.

After a short trip to our group in Hebden Bridge in Yorkshire, we were back in New York. It was just seven months after our last stay there. Once again we travelled up to Walden to see H.H. Sakya Trichen and, this time, to receive some short private teaching. When we had met the previous autumn, His Holiness had suggested that I come to receive Zhalu Losal Tenchong's text *A Condensed Method of the Practice of 'Showing the Dharmata'*, a brief but profound set of instructions on the view for Vajrayogini practitioners.

While in New York, I also gave two evenings of teachings at Tibet House on *The Three Visions*, and spent a very enjoyable afternoon with my friend Khenpo Pema Wangdak at his apartment on the Upper West Side – an apartment which doubles as the Palden Sakya Centre. It's not the largest of places, and as Albena and I were with three generations of our family, it was overflowing!

There were two European trips in June: Stuttgart and northern Italy. I had been invited by a Bodhi Path Centre located in the Alpine village of Bordo. The place had been semi-restored from dereliction by a group of German free spirits in the 1980s, and Shamar Rinpoche had folded it in to the Bodhi Path network in 2006. Now it was led by archaeologist-turned-nun, Tengye-la, who had, like many Bodhi Path teachers, been trained at Dhagpo Kundreul Ling. It is reached by a fairly alarming hike up the mountain, the last stretch of the journey being inaccessible to motor vehicles.

After completing my teaching there on the Four Limitless Meditations, we returned to London to receive Karma Thinley Rinpoche, who was stopping over, before journeying on to Kathmandu. Happily, on this occasion, he gave me the transmission for his newly composed text, *Sweet Drops of the Nectar of Great Bliss*, a commentary on *The Uncommon Sadhana of Vajrayogini*.

July began in Manchester with the *Jewel Ornament* and then, later that month, we travelled to France, where we would spend the next six weeks. Immediately after arriving, I commenced a new cycle of teaching at the Dhagpo Institute, on Sonam Tsemo's *General Presentation of the Tantra Sets*.

Before I could begin my scheduled teachings at Changlochen, we had something of an intermission, when Albena and I had to travel up to Antwerp in Belgium for the first ever European Sakya Monlam. Although the Sakya Monlam had been flourishing for over twenty years in Nepal, now, due to the very large numbers of Tibetan Sakya lay-followers residing in the West, the Phodrang had accepted the invitation to attend and lead similar gatherings in North America and Europe.

We had talked to the Phodrang about this and I had sent Wolfgang from Stuttgart, Dolma from Zurich and Benjamin from London to work in the organising committee. Accordingly, it was imperative for Albena and me to participate in this first three-day Monlam. The event itself was mainly attended by Tibetans, and perhaps a fifth of those present were Europeans. At the end of the three days, H.H. Sakya Gongma Trichen bestowed the long-life initiation of Tangtong Gyalpo.

It's obvious to me that His Holiness and my other masters have a deep and abiding concern for the welfare of their Tibetan followers. As I know from my conversations with them, they wish to see that the integrity of the Tibetan people and their culture be preserved. These Monlams held in the West are, at least, partially to aid the Tibetan diaspora to preserve its identity, as H.H. Ratna Rinpoche told me three years ago. The work currently being done both by H.H. Karmapa and H.H. Gyana Vajra Rinpoche in extending educational opportunities to children in the Himalayan region should also be seen as driven by the same concern.

It's important for those of us involved in the dharma in the West to acknowledge this concern and work, and take them seriously. We can sometimes be somewhat narrowly focussed just on the dharma in the West and our Tibetan masters' relationship with us. This might cause us to overlook the fact that our masters have a sense of responsibility towards the people of their nation. However, it's not one that contradicts their universal concern for all beings. It is simply a result of karma and vows that, right now, they have such connections, just as we do with our own families. As the dharma proclaims that one's journey to limitless love and compassion starts with those to whom we are presently intimately connected, perhaps we can learn from the example of our masters.

Back in the Dordogne, after Katharina had accomplished her first short retreat on White Saraswati, the goddess of wisdom and poetry, I spent a week at Changlochen teaching *Patterns in Emptiness*. In the second week there, I gave Tsembupa's tri on Chenrezi for the first time since I had received it seven years earlier. For those Sakya followers who don't have the time for such complex practices as Hevajra or Vajrayogini, this system provides an alternative and simpler method of accomplishing the preliminaries and the yogas of the development and completion stages.

We left France at the beginning of September but would be back within three weeks for the visit of H.H. Karmapa to Dhagpo. However, before that, I had to teach in Harrogate and Stuttgart. In the latter location, I gave the initiation of Bhutadamara together with Zhuchen Tsultrim Rinchen's guiding instructions. A day or two after Stuttgart, we were in a very wet Dhagpo, where H.H. Karmapa gave the Bodhisattva Vow and Chenrezi initiation to over three thousand people, a number which put a considerable strain on the facilities.

His Holiness taught in his ever fresh way, renewing the dharma for each individual present. Sometimes you might think that, in order to reach as many people as possible with his words, he is condensing or simplifying points, but, later, when you turn it over in your mind, you realise that it was simply a teaching on *Mahamudra* that was expressed in an unexpected manner. His Holiness is adept at presenting the profound truths of the Vajrayana in such a way that it's useful for those just setting out and those seemingly more learned. His mind is utterly spacious in this way. I was still thinking about this as we travelled to Karma Migyur Ling, where I had been asked to teach on *Patterns in Emptiness*.

October and November were relatively quiet with the Namgyalma and Sixteen Arhats initiations in Bristol and London, followed, in November, by further teachings in Prague and Manchester. After these trips, it was Bodhgaya, once again, for the International Karma-Kagyu Meeting. This year, the theme of transmission had been settled upon by H.H. Karmapa. Khenpo Chodrak Tenphel Rinpoche, one of the greatest scholars of the tradition, opened the meeting with his historical survey of Kagyu transmission. I was the final person to speak. My brief was to discuss issues affecting the lineage in the West, and, in particular, the danger of dilution. In this respect, I believe that it is crucial that what we teach is in accord with the intention of the sutras and tantras, for simply by the alteration of one key point, the power of the dharma to bring about liberation can be lost.

Of course, you can win your way to fortune and fame, if you know how to corrupt the dharma and flatter people. Nowadays, there are plenty of rich vampires and their corporations and foundations out there wanting to make a deal. They've been at work for quite some time in substituting Mara for Buddha here in the Buddhism of the West. However, for me, I couldn't join in with their schemes even if I wanted to do so – there are some things in life that it just gets too late to learn.

Immediately the Meeting finished, we travelled back to London to greet Karma Thinley Rinpoche on his way back to Toronto. After hosting Rinpoche for two days, during which time he gave part of the transmission for Kunu Rinpoche's *Praise of Bodhichitta*, we set off to spend two weeks in our place in the Dordogne.

My first trip of 2020 was then to Los Angeles, where I gave teachings on the *Eight Verses of Mind-Training* and the initiation of Chenrezi. After returning to England, I gave the initiation of Gonkar in Bristol. At the end of the month, we returned to Zurich for the first time in sixteen years. It was in response to a joint invitation from the local Bodhi Path group and Andrew and Dolma Gutmann, who had relocated there after a number of years in London. I taught *The Short Prayer to Vajradhara* and gave the transmission of Chenrezi. Some weeks later, the *Jewel Ornament of Liberation* continued in Manchester.

The next stops were Paris and Normandy. While we were there, I dreamed that we were in some town by the Pacific Ocean, where, by chance, we came across a Mongolian temple. As I was wondering whether we should go in, I suddenly found that I was inside, giving an initiation. In the middle of the ritual, an old scruffily dressed woman pushed to the front of the crowd and gave me a bunch of keys; they looked like car keys. I guessed that she wanted me to use them in the initiation but I've never heard of keys being used in an initiation. What's more, I don't drive a car.

It occurred to me that, as this was a Gelug place, perhaps they use such keys. However, I decided to carry on with the initiation in the usual style. I chanted the ancient familiar words, just as all those before me have done through the centuries, and threaded my rosary beads through my fingers. I took up my vajra and bell. Everything seemed to be working fine, and, as for the mystery of the keys, I'll figure it out somehow.

Lama Jampa Thaye
London, May 2020

Textual sources

Most of the initiations and transmissions mentioned in this history are found in the following major collections:

- A Collection of Sadhanas and Related Texts of the Vajrayana Tradition of Tibet (sgrub thabs kun btus). Collected by Jamyang Khyentse Wangpo and Jamgon Loter Wangpo. 14 volumes.

- The Treasury of Spiritual Instructions (gdams ngag mdzod). Collected by Jamgon Kongtrul Lodro Thaye. 18 volumes.

- The Collected Works of the Five Venerable Sakya Masters (sa skya'i bka' 'bum). 15 volumes.

- The Great Collection of the *Lamdre* (*Path and its Fruit*) (gsung ngag lam 'bras). 41 volumes.

- The Collected Works on Vajrayogini Sakyapa Tradition (dpal ldan sa skya pa'i lugs kyi na ro mkha' spyod ma'i lugs). 3 volumes.

- The Treasure of Ultimate Meaning, the Great Seal Teachings (nges don phyag rgya chen po'i khrid mdzod). 18 volumes.

- The Collection of Tantras (rgyud sde kun btus). Collected by Jamyang Khyentse Wangpo and Jamgon Loter Wangpo. 32 volumes.

Other texts mentioned in the history are either found as stand-alone editions published in Tibet, Nepal or India, or as one or more works in an individual master's Collected Works.

Works by Karma Thinley Rinpoche in Tibetan have been printed over the last three decades by Jetsunma Rigzin Khandro at Marpa Gompa in Canada.

There are a number of histories and biographies that provide useful background on some of the historical figures mentioned in this work:

- Dongthog Rinpoche, *The Sakya School of Tibetan Buddhism* (Wisdom Publications, Boston, 2016).

- Karma Thinley, *The 16 Karmapas of Tibet* (Prajna Press, Boulder, 1980).

- Dudjom Rinpoche, *The Nyingma School of Tibetan Buddhism* (Wisdom Publications, Boston, 1991).

- Alexander Gardner, *The Life of Jamgon Kongtrul the Great* (Snow Lion, Boulder, 2019).

- Richard Barron, *The Autobiography of Jamgon Kongtrul* (Snow Lion, Ithaca, 2003).

- Sam van Schaik, *Tibet: A History* (Yale University Press, London, 2010).

Notes

1   Tsar chen bLo gsal rGya mtsho, *Shes gnyen dam pa bsten par byed pa'i thabs shlo ka lnga bcu pa'i 'grel pa dngos grub rin po che'i sgo byed* in The Great Collection of the Lamdre, vol.20, (Sachen International, 2008), p.19.

2   Shantideva, op.cit. p.54B.

3   The 'four unbroken practices' are (i) the six-limbed sadhana of Hevajra, (ii) the uncommon daily sadhana of Vajrayogini, (iii) the Guru-Yoga of the Profound Path and (iv) Virupa's Protection.

4   dKon mchog rjes dran gyi mdo in *Varanasi sa skya pa'i zhal 'don phyogs bsdus* (Sarnath, 2001), p.3.

5   The papers from the conference were published in G.Samuel and J. Oliphant eds. *About Padmasambhava: Historical Narratives and Later Transformations of Guru Rinpoche* (Garuda Verlag, Schongau, 2020).

6   T.S. Eliot, 'Burnt Norton', in T.S. Eliot, *Collected Poems 1909-1962* (Harcourt, Inc., New York, 1963), p.178.

7 Shantideva, op. cit. p.14A.

8 Since the enthronement of H.H. the 42nd Sakya Trizin, Ratna Vajra Rinpoche, his father H.H. the 41st Sakya Trizin, who is referred to up to this point in this account as H.H. Sakya Trizin, is referred to as H.H. the 41st Sakya Gongma Trichen, or simply H.H. Sakya Trichen.

9 For a recent comment by H.H. Sakya Gongma Trichen, see *Buddhist Ethics* (Tsechen Kunchab Choling, Publications, Walden, New York, 2015), p.15.

Publishing finished
in July 2021 by Pulsio
Publisher Number: 4020
Legal Deposit: July 2021
Printed in Bulgaria